EARL EDWARDS

Retirement Reinvented

The Ultimate Playbook For Financial Freedom

Copyright © 2022 by Earl Edwards

All rights reserved. No part of this publication may be reproduced, stored or transmitted in any form or by any means, electronic, mechanical, photocopying, recording, scanning, or otherwise without written permission from the publisher. It is illegal to copy this book, post it to a website, or distribute it by any other means without permission.

First edition

*This book was professionally typeset on Reedsy.
Find out more at reedsy.com*

Contents

1	Introduction	1
2	The Shift in Retirement Paradigm	4
	The Changing Landscape of Retirement	7
	The Need for a New Approach	9
	The Rise of Financial Independence	12
	The New Retirement Framework	15
	Common Retirement Myths Debunked	18
	Embracing the New Retirement Paradigm	20
3	The Mindset of Financial Freedom	24
	Shifting from Scarcity to Abundance	24
	Taking Ownership of Your Financial Future	27
	Setting Clear Financial Goals	30
	Cultivating Financial Discipline and Habits	32
	Embracing Risk and Learning from Failure	35
	Adopting a Growth Mindset	37
	Cultivating Gratitude and Contentment	39
	Seeking Financial Education and Mentorship	42
	Nurturing a Positive Money Mindset	45
4	Unleashing Your True Potential	48
	Self-Reflection and Personal Assessment	48
	Discovering Your Passions and Purpose	51
	Capitalizing on Transferable Skills	53
	Pursuing Lifelong Learning	55
	Embracing Entrepreneurship	58

	Emphasizing Social Impact and Volunteerism	61
	Balancing Leisure and Productivity	63
	Embracing New Opportunities and Embracing Change	66
5	Income Generation Strategies	69
	The Power of Passive Income	69
	Real Estate Ventures	72
	Online Business and E-Commerce	74
	Creating and Monetizing Intellectual Property	77
	Freelancing and Consulting	79
	Investment Strategies for Retirement	81
	Entrepreneurship and Small Business Ventures	84
	Gig Economy and On-Demand Work	86
	Balancing Income and Lifestyle	88
6	Wealth Building and Investment Strategies	92
	The Power of Compound Interest	92
	Building a Diversified Investment Portfolio	94
	Setting Clear Investment Goals	97
	Understanding Risk and Reward	99
	Investing in Stocks and Equities	102
	Fixed Income Investments: Bonds and Treasury Securities	104
	Real Estate Investment Strategies	107
	Alternative Investments and Asset Classes	110
	Getting to know the unique qualities and risks	111
	Suitability and Portfolio Allocation	112
	Monitoring and Adjusting Your Portfolio	113
	Taking a disciplined approach to monitoring the portfolio	113
	How to Measure the Success of an Investment	114

Making the Needed Changes	115
7 Prioritizing Health and Wellness	117
The Importance of Physical Activity	117
Benefits of working out regularly	118
Looking at Different Kinds of Physical Activities	118
Creating a personalized workout plan	119
Healthy Eating and Nutrition	121
How nutrition affects health and happiness	121
Basics of a well-balanced and healthy diet	122
Getting into the habit of eating well	122
How to Choose Food Wisely	123
Mental and Cognitive Stimulation	124
Why Mental and Cognitive Stimulation is Important	124
Activities to keep your mind and brain active	125
Being aware and meditating	125
Social Connections and Relationships	126
Why it's important to have friends	127
Getting involved in social things	127
Keeping relationships that matter alive	128
Stress Management and Relaxation Techniques	129
Understanding Stress Management	129
Relaxation Techniques	130
Setting priorities for self-care	130
Sleep and Restorative Rest	131
How Important Good Sleep Is	132
Setting up good sleep habits	132
Getting Help from a Professional	133
Preventive Health Care and Regular Check-ups	134
Why preventive health care is important	134

	Healthcare Professionals to Consult	135
	Taking charge of long-term conditions	135
	Problems with health are dealt with quickly	136
	Active Lifestyle and Hobbies	137
	Advantages of living an active life	137
	Why it's good to have hobbies	138
	Getting a Good Balance	138
	Emotional Well-being and Self-Care	139
	How important emotional health is	140
	Benefits of doing things for yourself	140
	Seeking Support	141
8	Creating Your Legacy	143
	Defining Your Personal Legacy	143
	Thinking about Values, Principles, and Beliefs	144
	Finding the most important parts	144
	Getting Clear on the Effect You Want	144
	Volunteering and Philanthropy	145
	How to Figure Out What It Means	146
	Looking at the Options	146
	Giving your time, skills, and money	147
	Effects and Gains	147
	Mentoring and Sharing Knowledge	148
	How to Figure Out What It Means	148
	Looking at the Options	149
	Effective mentoring and sharing of knowledge	149
	The benefits and results	150
	Environmental Sustainability	151
	How to Figure Out What It Means	151
	Contributing to the preservation of the environment	151
	Getting the word out about environmental stewardship	152

The benefits and results	153
Artistic Expression and Creativity	154
Trying out artistic projects	154
Different ways to express art	154
Sharing Creative Works	155
Inspiring Future Generations	156
Getting in touch with younger people	157
What a mentor does	157
Getting people to think about growth and passion	158
Documenting Your Life Story	159
How to Keep Your Story	159
How to Write a Journal or Memoir	160
Telling the story of your life	160
Advocacy and Social Change	161
Why it's Important to Advocate	161
Using Your Voice to Make a Difference	162
How to Be Part of Social Change	162
Fostering Meaningful Relationships	163
Why meaningful relationships are important	164
Taking care of family ties	164
How to Make Good Friends	165
Putting together a support system	165
9 Frequently Asked Questions about Retirement	167
10 The Roadmap to Retirement Success	175
Define Your Retirement Vision	175
Thinking About the Life You Want	176
Making plans	176
Making a plan for retirement	177
Assess Your Financial Readiness	177

Think about how your money is going right now	178
Determine Your Retirement Income Needs	178
Calculate Your Retirement Savings	179
Get help from a professional	179
Develop a Retirement Income Strategy	180
Find Possible Ways to Make Money in Retirement	181
Create a Budget	181
Explore Strategies to Maximize Retirement Income	182
Plan for Healthcare and Long-Term Care	183
Check out your options and costs for health care	183
Think about insurance for long-term care	184
Make a plan for healthcare and long-term care management	185
Establish an Estate Plan	186
Talk to an attorney about estate planning	186
Choose the people who will benefit and plan for tax efficiency	187
Review and keep your will up to date	188
Embrace Lifestyle Choices	189
Think about how you'd like to spend your time	189
Do things that bring you joy and satisfaction	190
Foster connections and relationships with other people	190
Find a Good Middle Ground	191
Prioritize Health and Wellness	192
Choosing a healthy way of life	192

Adding Activities for Mental and Emotional Health		193
Stay Engaged and Connected		194
Build Relationships That Matter		194
Family and Friends: Make it a priority to care for and improve your ties with your family and close friends. Spend valuable time together, talk to each other often, and make memories that will last. Do things that bring you closer together and help you understand each other, like sharing meals, trips, or holidays.		194
Do things with other people		195
Keep up with news and get involved		195
Adapt and Adjust		196
Continuous Evaluation		196
Making the Needed Changes		197
Looking for Help and Direction		197
11	Conclusion	199
12	Retirement Action Plan Worksheet	201

1

Introduction

Retirement is a time of great anticipation and dreams. It's the phase of life where you finally get to relax, enjoy the fruits of your labor, and pursue your passions. However, the traditional retirement plans that have been passed down for generations are no longer sufficient in today's rapidly changing world.

"Retirement Reinvented: The Ultimate New Playbook for Financial Freedom" is your guide to a brighter and more fulfilling retirement. In this comprehensive ebook, we will explore the shifting paradigms of retirement and introduce you to an innovative approach that will empower you to take charge of your financial future.

Gone are the days of relying solely on a pension or Social Security to sustain you through your golden years. This book will open your eyes to new possibilities and equip you with the knowledge and strategies to build a retirement plan that aligns with your unique goals and aspirations.

We will delve into the importance of cultivating a mindset of financial freedom and explore how it can transform your relationship with money. You will discover the power of income generation strategies that go beyond traditional employment, allowing you to create multiple streams of income and achieve true financial independence.

Investing wisely is another key aspect of "Retirement Reinvented: The Ultimate New Playbook for Financial Freedom." We will unveil smart investment principles that will help you grow your wealth and secure a prosperous future. You'll gain insights into the world of entrepreneurship, passive income, and other innovative investment opportunities.

But retirement is about more than just money. It's about designing a lifestyle that brings you joy, fulfillment, and purpose. We will guide you through the process of lifestyle design, enabling you to envision and create the retirement you've always dreamed of.

Health and wellness are vital components of a happy retirement. We will explore strategies for maintaining your wellbeing and maximizing your physical and mental health as you age gracefully.

Navigating the complexities of Social Security and Medicare can be overwhelming. Fear not! This book will provide you with valuable insights and practical advice to help you make informed decisions and optimize your benefits.

INTRODUCTION

Creating a lasting legacy is something many of us aspire to. We will dive into legacy planning and estate strategies, ensuring that your wealth and values are passed down to future generations.

Throughout "Retirement Reinvented: The Ultimate New Playbook for Financial Freedom," we will address common challenges faced during retirement and equip you with the tools to overcome them. From relationships and adapting to change to the power of networking and embracing technology, you'll be prepared for any curveball life throws your way.

To ensure we cover all your burning questions, we've dedicated an entire chapter to answering the top 30 questions people ask about retirement planning and financial security.

Lastly, we'll guide you in creating your action plan, a step-by-step roadmap that will turn your newfound knowledge into tangible results. By the end of this book, you'll be equipped with a personalized retirement plan that guarantees a prosperous and fulfilling future.

It's time to embrace "Retirement Reinvented: The Ultimate New Playbook for Financial Freedom" and embark on a journey of financial freedom, purpose, and joy. Your golden years await!

2

The Shift in Retirement Paradigm

Retirement has changed a lot over the years, which is a reflection of how our society has changed and how people's wants have changed in the modern world. Traditional plans for retirement, which were once thought to be good, have slowly lost their value. This chapter looks at how the way people think about retirement is changing and why traditional retirement plans no longer work in today's world.

In the past, people often thought of retirement as a time when they would stop working for good and take a well-deserved break. People used to depend on company benefits and social security from the government to keep themselves financially stable. But retirement has changed over time due to a number of reasons, and the traditional way of doing things needs to be rethought.

The fact that people are living longer is a big reason for

this change. People now live longer, healthier lives because medicine has gotten better and living situations have gotten better. Because of this, people are living in retirement longer, which means they need more money to support themselves for a longer time. Traditional retirement plans, which were made for people who were only going to be retired for a short time, may not be enough to meet the financial needs of people in the modern world.

The changing nature of work is also an important issue. Less and less people work for the same company for their whole lives like they used to. A lot of people now switch careers, work for themselves for a while, or do independent work. The gig economy and the rise of working from home have made the shift between working and retiring easier. In a world where people have more freedom and control over their jobs, the traditional idea of retiring at a certain age with a set income becomes less important.

Also, people's goals and ideas about retirement have changed over time. Many people no longer think of retirement as just a time to chill out and do nothing. Instead, they want to be happy, have a reason, and keep doing things that matter. This change in how people think has led to the rise of "second acts," or "encore careers," in which people follow new interests, start businesses, or do volunteer work after leaving their main jobs.

Traditional retirement plans, which are mostly about making sure you have enough money, might not be able to keep up with these changing goals and the desire for a more active and meaningful retirement.

Also, there have been big changes in the way the economy works. Globalization, changes in the economy, and financial disasters have all had an effect on how stable pension systems and social security programs are. Because of this, people now have more responsibility for how they manage their investments and savings for retirement. Traditional retirement plans that rely on money from outside sources may no longer be enough to guarantee a happy retirement.

Because of these changes, new ways of planning for retirement have come about. People are urged to save and invest for their futures in a more active way. Individual Retirement Accounts (IRAs) and 401(k) plans are popular ways to save for retirement. This is because they give people more power and flexibility over their money. Also, there is a greater focus on financial literacy and education to give people the tools they need to make smart choices about their retirement savings.

In a nutshell, retirement has changed a lot over the years because of changes in society, the economy, and culture. Even though traditional retirement plans worked well in the past, they don't meet the wants and expectations of people today. The idea of retirement has changed because people are living longer, their jobs are changing, their goals are changing, and the economy is unclear. As time goes on, it is important to change retirement planning methods to keep up with these changes and make sure that people in the 21st century can have a safe and fulfilling retirement.

The Changing Landscape of Retirement

People used to think of retirement as a simple and regular time of life, but that has changed a lot in recent years. The old way of planning for retirement, which relied on benefits and a set retirement age, isn't as good as it used to be because of changes in the economy and society. This chapter looks at the changing nature of retirement from a historical, economic, and social point of view, as well as the decline of standard pensions.

In the past, retirement was often seen as the end of a person's working life and a time to rest and relax after years of hard work. People would plan for retirement by putting money into pension funds or depending on retirement plans offered by their employers. These plans gave retirees a steady source of income that they could count on, giving them a sense of security and financial stability. But this way of planning for retirement was based on some ideas that no longer hold true.

The fact that people are living longer plays a big role in how they plan for retirement. Better health care and better living situations have made people live longer. This is definitely a good thing, but it also means that people now have to plan for a retirement that could last several decades. The amount of money needed to support oneself for such a long time has grown, making it harder for standard retirement plans that were made for shorter retirement periods to work.

Also, rising health care costs are a big problem for saving for retirement. As people live longer, they are more likely to have health problems and need medical care. If you don't plan for them well, healthcare costs like insurance premiums, drug costs, and long-term care can quickly wipe out your retirement savings. Healthcare prices have become a very important thing to think about when planning for retirement in the modern world.

Changes have also happened in the job market, which affects how people plan for retirement. The old idea that you would work for one company for the rest of your life has been replaced by a job market that is more active and fluid. People can change jobs, work for themselves or as freelancers for a while, or work part-time during their retirement years. Because of how work is changing, the line between working and retiring is becoming less clear. This makes the change between the two more gradual and fluid. Because of this, the idea of a set retirement age and stopping all work is becoming less important.

The decline of standard pension plans is another important change. Many companies have moved away from defined benefit pension plans, which give a fixed income in retirement, in favor of defined contribution plans like 401(k)s. With this change, it is up to the person to plan for retirement and decide how to invest. Defined contribution plans give you more control and freedom, but they also bring more risk and uncertainty. Due to the decline of standard pensions, people have had to look for other ways to pay for their retirement, such as savings, investments, and Social Security.

The world of aging has changed a lot over the past few years. Changes in the economy and society, like longer life expectancy, higher health care costs, and changes in the job market, have made it harder for standard retirement planning to work. The decline of standard pensions has made it even more important for people to plan and save for their retirement on their own. As people try to figure out how to live in this changing world, it's important to think about things like longer life spans, higher health care costs, and other ways to make money. Keeping up with these changes is important if you want to have a safe and happy retirement in the modern world.

The Need for a New Approach

In the current world, planning for retirement needs a new point of view. Traditional means, like Social Security payments, are no longer enough to guarantee a safe and happy retirement. This chapter talks about how uncertain social security is, how savings alone aren't enough, and how the desire for a busy and purpose-driven retirement is growing.

One of the hardest things about planning for retirement is not knowing what will happen with social security. Social Security has been a very important safety net for retirees, but its limits are becoming more and more clear. The growing population and changes in the way people live have put pressure on the social security system and made people worry about its long-term viability. Also, the future of social security benefits is still unclear, since the program may need to be changed or fixed to make up for budget shortfalls. People who depend only on social security benefits for their retirement income risk having their benefits cut or other changes made that could hurt their finances.

Another important thing to think about is that savings alone are not enough. Personal savings are a key part of a person's retirement income and help keep them financially stable in their later years. But studies have shown that many people don't have enough money saved to support themselves in retirement. Depending only on savings may not be a good idea if you don't save enough, have unexpected costs, or don't get the best return on your investments. To deal with this problem, it is important for people to start saving for retirement as soon as possible and to use methods that encourage long-term growth and financial stability.

Also, more and more people want to spend their retirement years doing things that give them a sense of meaning. The usual idea of retirement as a time to stop working completely and do nothing is slowly going away. Many seniors today are looking for ways to stay active, follow their own interests, and give back to their communities. People are becoming more interested in active retirement because they want to feel fulfilled, keep learning, and spend time with other people. It shows that we need a new way to plan for retirement that takes into account how important it is to keep living an active, meaningful life after we retire.

Because of these things, planning for retirement needs to be done differently. People should think about a plan that includes more than one way to make money. This could include income from Social Security, personal funds, investments, and even part-time work or starting a business during retirement. By having more than one source of income, people can avoid the risks that come with depending on just one. This gives them more financial stability and freedom.

Also, financial literacy and education must be a top priority in order to give people the information and skills they need to plan for retirement well. Understanding how to invest, keep track of costs, and get the most out of retirement benefits can have a big impact on a retiree's long-term financial health. By teaching people about money, they can make smart choices, save as much as they can for retirement, and adjust to changes in the economy.

Also, people should do what they can to improve their health and well-being when they leave. Regular exercise, keeping a healthy lifestyle, and pursuing personal hobbies can all help make retirement enjoyable and fulfilling. By putting their physical and mental health first, people can improve their quality of life and live longer in retirement.

To use this new method, people should deal with the unknowns about social security in a responsible way. Even though it's smart to count social security benefits in retirement income figures, it's also important to think about other ways to make money to make up for any changes or cuts to social security benefits. This could mean looking into investments like stocks, bonds, or real estate that have the ability to grow and bring in money over time.

Building up your own savings is another important part of the new way to plan for retirement. Instead of depending only on retirement plans offered by their employers, people should develop a disciplined savings plan that helps them build up wealth over time. By consistently setting aside a part of their income and using tax-advantaged savings accounts like individual retirement accounts (IRAs) or Roth IRAs, people can strengthen their financial foundation and be more financially independent in retirement.

Also, getting help from financial advisors, retirement planners, and health care workers can be a huge help for people trying to figure out how to plan for retirement. These experts can give useful insights, give personalized advice, and help come up with strategies that fit the goals and circumstances of each person.

In the end, the changing nature of retirement means that preparation needs to be done differently. Relying only on Social Security payments, not saving enough, or living a sedentary life in retirement are no longer good choices. People should instead adopt a complete plan that includes multiple sources of income, puts financial literacy first, encourages an active, purpose-driven lifestyle, and puts an emphasis on health and well-being as a whole. By planning for retirement in a proactive and all-around way, people can make sure they have a secure, fulfilling, and financially stable retirement that fits their own goals and wishes.

The Rise of Financial Independence

Financial independence and early retirement have gained considerable attention in recent years, inspiring individuals to reimagine their relationship with work and wealth. This chapter explores the concept of financial independence, its association with early retirement, and the increasing popularity of the Financial Independence, Retire Early (FIRE) movement.

Financial Independence and Early Retirement: Financial independence refers to achieving a state where individuals have accumulated sufficient wealth and passive income streams to cover their living expenses without the need for traditional employment. It entails attaining a level of financial freedom that allows individuals to have more control over their time and pursue activities that align with their passions and values. Early retirement, on the other hand, involves leaving the workforce at a younger age than traditionally expected, leveraging financial independence to sustain a fulfilling lifestyle.

The FIRE Movement: The Financial Independence, Retire Early (FIRE) movement has gained momentum in recent years, capturing the attention and aspirations of many individuals seeking an alternative approach to traditional retirement. The principles of FIRE revolve around maximizing savings, reducing expenses, and making intentional lifestyle choices to achieve financial independence at an earlier stage of life.

FIRE adherents adopt frugality as a core principle, diligently saving a significant portion of their income while minimizing unnecessary expenses. By living below their means and directing savings towards investments, they aim to accumulate wealth at an accelerated pace. This disciplined approach often involves optimizing spending, eliminating debt, and prioritizing investments with the potential for long-term growth.

Central to the FIRE movement is the notion of retiring early, which does not necessarily mean complete withdrawal from work but rather having the freedom to choose how and when to engage in employment. Early retirees can pursue part-time work, passion projects, or entrepreneurial endeavors that align with their interests and provide fulfillment beyond financial compensation.

The growing popularity of FIRE can be attributed to several

factors. First, it represents a response to societal shifts and changing attitudes towards work and retirement. Many individuals are seeking alternatives to the traditional notion of spending the majority of their lives in employment, with retirement as the sole period of rest and leisure. FIRE offers an opportunity to realign work and lifestyle choices, promoting a more balanced and fulfilling existence.

Moreover, the accessibility of information and online communities has fueled the spread of FIRE principles. Online platforms, forums, and blogs dedicated to financial independence and early retirement have created a supportive network where individuals can share experiences, strategies, and success stories. This sense of community and shared knowledge has inspired and empowered many to pursue their path towards financial independence.

However, it is important to recognize that FIRE is not without its challenges and criticisms. Critics argue that the principles of extreme frugality and aggressive savings may not be feasible or desirable for everyone. It requires discipline, long-term planning, and the ability to navigate potential economic uncertainties. Additionally, the emphasis on early retirement may not align with everyone's personal and professional aspirations, as some individuals find meaning and fulfillment in their chosen careers.

Financial independence and early retirement have emerged as a popular concept, challenging traditional notions of work and retirement. The Financial Independence, Retire Early (FIRE) movement offers a roadmap for achieving financial freedom and pursuing a lifestyle that prioritizes personal fulfillment and autonomy. While FIRE is not without its critics and challenges, it has inspired many individuals to reevaluate their relationship with money, work, and the pursuit of a meaningful life. As more people embrace the principles of financial independence, the landscape of retirement continues to evolve, providing individuals with new opportunities and choices to shape their futures.

The New Retirement Framework

In the past, planning for retirement has mostly been about making sure you have enough money. But in the modern world, it's important to look at retirement as a whole in order to have a happy and fulfilling life after work. This chapter talks about a new way to think about retirement that focuses on finding a balance between financial security, health and wellness, personal satisfaction, and social connections. By being proactive and flexible, people can handle the challenges of retirement and build a meaningful and successful life after they stop working.

A Whole-Brain Approach to Planning for Retirement: The new retirement framework looks at more than just money. It takes into account how different parts of life are linked. It recognizes that a happy retirement is about more than just having enough money. So, planning for retirement should include ways to stay healthy physically and mentally, follow personal interests, and make new friends. People can have a peaceful and healthy retirement if they look at the whole picture.

Finding a balance between financial security, health and

wellness, personal happiness, and social connections: In the new system, financial stability is still a key part of planning for retirement. It means making a solid financial plan that includes savings, investments, and sources of income to support the living one wants. Proper financial planning gives people peace of mind and lets them focus on other parts of retirement without constantly worrying about money.

Along with financial stability, it's important to put health and fitness first. Retirement gives you the chance to take care of yourself, start healthy habits, and exercise regularly. By taking care of their physical and mental health, people can improve their quality of life, keep their independence, and have a full and busy retirement.

Personal satisfaction is another important part of the new retirement plan. Retirement gives you the chance to do things you've always wanted to do, find new things you're interested in, and spend time on your own growth and self-discovery. People in retirement should actively look for things that bring them joy, meaning, and a sense of purpose. This could mean doing something creative, going back to school, or trying something new.

Social connections play a vital part in retirement. Having good ties with family, friends, and the community is a big part of being happy and healthy in general. When you retire, you have the time and energy to invest in these relationships, take part in social events, and give back to the community. Building and keeping a network of support makes retirement more enjoyable and helps fight feelings of separation or loneliness.

Adopting a proactive and flexible mindset: For retirement to go well, you need to be proactive and flexible. People should be ready to accept change, try out new options, and change their plans as things change. Retirement is not a stage that stays the same, but a journey that changes over time. Being open to new experiences and tasks can help you grow as a person and have a fulfilling life after you retire.

It's important to stay interested and curious. Continuous growth and brain stimulation come from learning new things, keeping up with current trends, and looking for ways to improve yourself. By being proactive and flexible, people can take advantage of chances, get past problems, and get the most out of their retirement years.

The new retirement framework includes a whole-person approach that includes financial stability, health and wellness, personal satisfaction, and social connections. People can have a happy and meaningful retirement by balancing these things and having a proactive and flexible mindset. This all-around method recognizes that retirement is a complex time of life that needs careful planning and ongoing participation. By using the new retirement framework, people can confidently handle the many challenges of retirement and have a happy and successful life after work.

Common Retirement Myths Debunked

There are a lot of myths and misunderstandings about retirement that shape how we think about it and what we expect from it. It is important to bust these myths so that we can make smart decisions and rethink retirement on our own terms. The goal of this chapter is to debunk some of the most popular retirement myths about the age of retirement, work vs. play, and being financially dependent. By going against what most people do, people can build a retirement that fits their own goals and desires.

Myths about the age of retirement:
One of the most common myths is that you have to be a certain age to quit. But the age of retirement shouldn't be set in stone. Instead, it should depend on each person's situation and goals. Some people may decide to quit early, while others may keep working past the age when most people retire. The key to figuring out when to retire is to think about your cash situation, your health, and what makes you happy. By putting an end to the myth about retirement age, people can decide when to quit based on their own unique situations.

The pleasure vs. Work Myth:
Another common retirement myth is that retirement is all about pleasure and not having to work at all. Even though leisure and relaxation are important parts of retirement, many people find meaning and satisfaction by continuing to work or work on worthwhile projects. Some people may choose to do part-time work, consulting, or start their own business

after they quit. By debunking the idea that work is better than leisure, people can rethink retirement as a time when work and leisure can go hand in hand, allowing for personal growth, contribution, and financial security.

Debunking the Financial Dependence Myth:

Having to rely on money in retirement is a worry that often causes fear and anxiety. But it's not true that retirement means you have to count on other people for money. People can be financially independent in retirement if they plan well and make smart choices with their money. This means making a strong plan for saving for retirement, looking into different investment choices, and living within one's means. By putting an end to the idea that people are financially dependent on other people, people can take steps toward financial security and peace of mind in retirement.

Putting Your Own Spin on Retirement:

By debunking common retirement myths, people can make their own decisions about what retirement means to them. It gives them the power to make decisions that fit with their own beliefs, goals, and situations. Retirement is not the same for everyone, and it shouldn't be based on what other people do. People can make a retirement plan that fits their own goals, hobbies, and passions if they accept the idea that retirement is a personal journey. Redefining retirement on one's own terms can lead to a more fulfilling and purpose-driven life after work, whether it's through a phased retirement, a new job path, or volunteer work.

Common retirement myths need to be debunked so that people can make smart choices and plan a retirement that fits their needs and wants. By debunking the retirement age myth, the "leisure vs. work" myth, and the "financial dependence" myth, people can change their own ideas about retirement. This lets them make decisions that are in line with their personal goals, financial goals, and general health. Retirement should be a time of self-discovery, growth, and fulfillment. By debunking these myths, people can embrace their own unique retirement path.

Embracing the New Retirement Paradigm

No longer is retirement a one-size-fits-all idea, and a new way of thinking about retirement is taking shape. This article looks at the most important things you need to do to embrace this new retirement paradigm, such as getting over your fear of change and welcoming it, taking responsibility for your own retirement journey, and planning for the long term. By following these rules, people can confidently navigate the changing world of retirement and build a fulfilling life after they stop working.

Overcoming Fear and Embracing Change:
When people think about retiring, they often feel afraid because it means making a big change from the known world of work to the unknown world of leisure and personal satisfaction. But to accept the new way of thinking about retirement, you have to get over your fear of change and embrace it. It means realizing that retirement is a chance to

grow, learn more about yourself, and try new things. People can approach retirement with excitement and a sense of adventure by rephrasing their fears as joy and by being open to the new opportunities it brings.

Taking Responsibility for Your Retirement Journey:
In the new way of thinking about retirement, people are urged to take responsibility for their retirement journey. This means taking an active role in making plans and making decisions. Retirement isn't something that just comes to us; it's a time in our lives that we can shape and make what we want it to be. By taking responsibility, people can set their retiring goals, figure out the steps they need to take to reach them, and make choices that are in line with their values and wants.

Taking responsibility also means being proactive about looking for chances and making the retirement lifestyle you want. It could mean trying out new hobbies, learning new skills, or starting your own business. By being involved in how their retirement turns out, people can develop a sense of meaning, fulfillment, and personal happiness.

Adopting a Long-Term View and Making Plans Ahead of Time:
The new retirement paradigm urges people to take a long-term view and make plans ahead of time. Retirement is not just a destination; it is a trip that spans several decades. People can make smart choices about their financial security, health, and overall well-being in retirement if they look at the big picture.

Setting goals, making a plan for saving for retirement, and

regularly reviewing and changing the plan as things change are all parts of proactive planning. To do this, you need to stay up-to-date on financial options, health care issues, and living choices that affect retirement. By being proactive, people can plan for problems, seize chances, and make changes to make sure their retirement is smooth and full.

Also, planning ahead means thinking about possible risks and possibilities. This could mean planning for unexpected health care bills, making an estate plan, or thinking about options for long-term care. By taking care of these worries ahead of time, people can protect their retirement and have peace of mind knowing they are ready for any future problems.

To embrace the new retirement paradigm, people need to get over their fears, take responsibility for their retirement journey, and plan for the long run. By following these rules, people can find their way through the changing world of retirement and build a life after work that is full, meaningful, and personally satisfying. Retirement is no longer a time to sit back and do nothing; it's a chance to shape one's future and look forward to all the possibilities. By embracing the new retirement paradigm, people can start an exciting journey of self-discovery, growth, and satisfaction in their golden years.

In this chapter, we have laid the foundation for the new retirement paradigm. By understanding the shifting landscape and redefining retirement goals, you are now prepared to embark on a transformative journey towards financial independence, personal fulfillment, and a retirement plan that truly reflects your dreams and aspirations.

Continue reading in Chapter 2: The Mindset of Financial Freedom.

3

The Mindset of Financial Freedom

In Chapter 2, we delve into the crucial aspect of developing the right mindset for financial freedom. A mindset shift is essential to embrace the principles and practices that lead to a secure and abundant retirement. Let's explore the key elements of cultivating a mindset of financial freedom.

Shifting from Scarcity to Abundance

We often look at retirement through the lens of scarcity, which leads to limiting ideas and a feeling of lack. But by noticing and questioning these thought patterns, people can change to a way of thinking that is more open to possibilities and chances. This chapter talks about how important it is to move from a mindset of scarcity to one of abundance in retirement. It talks about how to recognize and challenge scarcity-based thinking patterns, adopt an abundance mindset, and get over limiting views about money and retirement.

Seeing and fighting scarcity-based ways of thinking:
Scarcity-based thinking comes from a lack of confidence and a focus on what is missing or not enough. When it comes to retirement, it usually shows up as worries about not having enough money, resources, or chances. The first step toward having an abundance mindset is to notice and question these ways of thought. It means being aware of negative thoughts and rethinking them in ways that are more positive and helpful.

Instead of focusing on how little money they have, people can think about their assets, skills, and strengths. By changing their attitude from one of lack to one of gratitude for what they have, people can start to see opportunities and possibilities they had not seen before. By challenging scarcity-based thinking, people can be more open to new ideas and ways of doing things. This lays the groundwork for an abundance attitude.

Having a wealth Mindset:
To have a wealth mindset, you need to believe that life is already full of good things. It acknowledges that there are plenty of chances, resources, and options, even after retirement. With an abundance attitude, problems are seen as chances to grow and learn. It teaches people to have a positive attitude and see setbacks as temporary and mistakes as steps on the way to success.

In the context of retirement, having an abundance mindset lets people change their focus from the lack of time, relationships, and personal satisfaction to the excess of those things. It encourages people to try new things, follow their interests, and look for ways to grow and help others. By having an abundance attitude, people can look forward to retirement with hope, curiosity, and excitement.

Overcoming Limiting Beliefs about Money and Retirement:
People can't have an abundance attitude if they have limiting beliefs about money and retirement. Beliefs like "I'll never have enough money to retire comfortably" or "Retiring means giving up financial security" can make people feel like they don't have enough and make them afraid. To have an abundance attitude, you must get rid of these limiting beliefs.

People can get rid of limiting ideas by challenging and reframing their thoughts. They can look for proof from people who have retired well and made a lot of money after they stopped working. People can also feel more in control and confident about their financial futures by doing financial planning, getting help from professionals, and learning about their investment choices. People can break free from scarcity-based thinking and enjoy all that retirement has to offer if they face their limiting beliefs head-on.

To move from a scarcity-based way of thinking to an abundance-based way of thinking in retirement, you have to recognize and challenge scarcity-based ways of thinking, adopt an abundance-based way of thinking, and get over limiting views about money and retirement. People can open themselves up to a world of possibilities and opportunities in retirement by changing the way they think, focusing on gratitude, and developing a positive attitude. When people have an abundance attitude, they feel like they have plenty of time, relationships, and personal fulfillment in retirement. By welcoming abundance, people can build a truly fulfilling and successful life after they retire.

Taking Ownership of Your Financial Future

Taking charge of your financial future is one of the most important things you can do to make sure you have a safe and successful retirement. It means realizing how important personal responsibility is in financial planning, giving yourself the information you need to make smart choices about saving, buying, and spending, and taking steps to make sure your financial future is safe. This chapter talks about how important it is to take charge of your financial future and gives key steps you can take to have a more safe and enjoyable retirement.

How to Figure Out How Much Personal Responsibility Matters in Financial Planning:

Personal duty is what makes good financial planning possible. It means realizing that you are in charge of your financial future and that what you do and decide today will affect your retirement tomorrow. By knowing how important it is to be responsible for yourself, you take charge of your financial well-being and make a promise to make decisions that help you reach your long-term goals.

Personal responsibility in financial planning means taking an active role in your funds, keeping track of your spending, and setting savings goals that are reasonable. It means learning about money, getting help from a professional when you need it, and keeping an eye on your finances and changing your plans as your life changes. By taking charge of your financial future, you become an active part of making your retirement what you want it to be.

Getting the information you need to make good decisions is a key part of taking charge of your financial future. It means getting the knowledge and information you need to make smart choices about saving, spending, and investment. If you know the basics of money, like how to make a budget, deal with debt, and invest, you can handle the complicated world of personal finances with ease.

Empowerment also means staying up-to-date on economic trends, planning choices for retirement, and changes to financial rules. By staying informed, you can make smart choices that help you reach your goals and adjust to changes in the financial world. Also, getting advice from people who work in finance can give you valuable information and help you make well-informed choices based on your unique situation.

Taking Proactive Steps to Secure Your Financial Future:

Taking charge of your financial future means taking proactive steps to secure your retirement. This means making a complete plan for your money that includes saving, investing, and paying off debt. You can keep track of your success and make changes as needed if you have clear goals and a plan.

Diversifying your investments is also a way to reduce risk and get the most out of your assets. It means that you should look at and adjust your investment account on a regular basis to make sure it fits your risk tolerance and your changing circumstances. Also, looking into ways to save for retirement, like Individual Retirement Accounts (IRAs) or employer-sponsored retirement plans, can help you save on taxes and secure your financial future.

Another step you can take to be responsible is to put savings first and live within your means. By making a budget, cutting expenses that aren't necessary, and saving a part of your income every month, you can build a strong base for your retirement. Being proactive also means dealing with any financial problems or failures right away, looking for ways to fix them, and changing your financial plans as needed.

Taking charge of your financial future is one of the most important things you can do to make sure you have a safe and successful retirement. By realizing how important personal responsibility is in financial planning, giving yourself the tools to make smart choices, and taking action, you can set yourself up for a more safe and enjoyable retirement. Remember that you are in charge of your own financial future. If you take charge, you can create a retirement that fits your goals, ambitions, and desired way of life. Start today, accept personal responsibility, and do things to make your financial future better.

Setting Clear Financial Goals

Taking charge of your financial future is one of the most important things you can do to make sure you have a safe and successful retirement. It means realizing how important personal responsibility is in financial planning, giving yourself the information you need to make smart choices about saving, buying, and spending, and taking steps to make sure your financial future is safe. This chapter talks about how important it is to take charge of your financial future and gives key steps you can take to have a more safe and enjoyable retirement.

How to Figure Out How Much Personal Responsibility Matters in Financial Planning:
Personal duty is what makes good financial planning possible. It means realizing that you are in charge of your financial future and that what you do and decide today will affect your retirement tomorrow. By knowing how important it is to be responsible for yourself, you take charge of your financial well-being and make a promise to make decisions that help you reach your long-term goals.

Personal responsibility in financial planning means taking an active role in your funds, keeping track of your spending, and setting savings goals that are reasonable. It means learning about money, getting help from a professional when you need it, and keeping an eye on your finances and changing your plans as your life changes. By taking charge of your financial future, you become an active part of making your retirement what you want it to be.

Getting the information you need to make good decisions is a key part of taking charge of your financial future. It means getting the knowledge and information you need to make smart choices about saving, spending, and investment. If you know the basics of money, like how to make a budget, deal with debt, and invest, you can handle the complicated world of personal finances with ease.

Empowerment also means staying up-to-date on economic trends, planning choices for retirement, and changes to financial rules. By staying informed, you can make smart choices that help you reach your goals and adjust to changes in the financial world. Also, getting advice from people who work in finance can give you valuable information and help you make well-informed choices based on your unique situation.

Taking Proactive Steps to Secure Your Financial Future:
Taking charge of your financial future means taking proactive steps to secure your retirement. This means making a complete plan for your money that includes saving, investing, and paying off debt. You can keep track of your success and make changes as needed if you have clear goals and a plan.

Diversifying your investments is also a way to reduce risk and get the most out of your assets. It means that you should look at and adjust your investment account on a regular basis to make sure it fits your risk tolerance and your changing circumstances. Also, looking into ways to save for retirement, like Individual Retirement Accounts (IRAs) or employer-sponsored retirement plans, can help you save on taxes and secure your financial future.

Another step you can take to be responsible is to put savings first and live within your means. By making a budget, cutting expenses that aren't necessary, and saving a part of your income every month, you can build a strong base for your retirement. Being proactive also means dealing with any financial problems or failures right away, looking for ways to fix them, and changing your financial plans as needed.

Taking charge of your financial future is one of the most important things you can do to make sure you have a safe and successful retirement. By realizing how important personal responsibility is in financial planning, giving yourself the tools to make smart choices, and taking action, you can set yourself up for a more safe and enjoyable retirement. Remember that you are in charge of your own financial future. If you take charge, you can create a retirement that fits your goals, ambitions, and desired way of life. Start today, accept personal responsibility, and do things to make your financial future better.

Cultivating Financial Discipline and Habits

Cultivating financial discipline and habits is crucial for achieving long-term financial stability and a successful retirement. It involves developing healthy financial habits, practicing delayed gratification, and creating a savings and investment strategy that aligns with your retirement goals. This chapter explores the importance of cultivating financial discipline and habits, including budgeting and expense tracking, practicing delayed gratification, and implementing an effective savings and investment strategy.

Developing Healthy Financial Habits:

One of the foundational financial habits is budgeting. Creating a budget allows you to have a clear understanding of your income, expenses, and financial obligations. By setting spending limits for different categories and tracking your expenses, you gain control over your financial decisions and identify areas where adjustments can be made.

Budgeting helps you prioritize your expenses, distinguishing between needs and wants. It enables you to allocate funds towards your retirement goals, such as savings and investments, while still meeting your essential needs. Regularly reviewing your budget and adjusting it as necessary ensures that you stay on track towards your financial objectives.

In addition to budgeting, tracking your expenses is essential for cultivating financial discipline. By monitoring your spending habits, you become more conscious of where your money is going and can identify areas where you may be overspending. Tracking expenses allows you to make informed decisions, make necessary adjustments, and avoid unnecessary financial strain.

Practicing Delayed Gratification and Avoiding Unnecessary Debt:

Practicing delayed gratification is a vital aspect of financial discipline. It involves resisting impulsive purchases and prioritizing long-term financial goals over short-term desires. By delaying immediate gratification, you can allocate funds towards savings and investments that will benefit you in the future.

Avoiding unnecessary debt is another key component of financial discipline. Debt, particularly high-interest debt, can hinder your ability to save for retirement and limit your financial freedom. Cultivating the habit of living within your means and avoiding unnecessary debt allows you to maintain financial stability and allocate more resources towards securing your retirement.

Creating a Savings and Investment Strategy:

A well-defined savings and investment strategy is essential for achieving retirement goals. It involves setting aside a portion of your income specifically for retirement savings. By automating savings contributions, you make it easier to remain consistent and disciplined with your saving habits.

Alongside savings, implementing an effective investment strategy is crucial for long-term growth and maximizing returns. Consider your risk tolerance, time horizon, and retirement goals when selecting investment vehicles. Diversifying your investments helps spread risk and increase the potential for returns.

Regularly reviewing and adjusting your savings and investment strategy is important as market conditions and personal circumstances change. Seeking advice from financial professionals can provide valuable insights and ensure that your strategy aligns with your retirement goals.

Cultivating financial discipline and habits is instrumental in achieving long-term financial stability and a successful retirement. By developing healthy financial habits such as budgeting and expense tracking, practicing delayed gratification, and implementing a savings and investment strategy, individuals can strengthen their financial foundation and work towards their retirement goals. Remember, financial discipline is a lifelong practice, requiring consistency and commitment. By cultivating these habits, you can confidently navigate your financial journey and create a secure and fulfilling retirement.

Embracing Risk and Learning from Failure

Embracing risk and learning from failure are essential aspects of wealth creation and retirement planning. Understanding the role of risk, overcoming the fear of failure, and being willing to take calculated risks are all integral to achieving long-term financial success. This chapter explores the significance of embracing risk and learning from failure in the context of wealth creation and retirement planning. By understanding these principles, individuals can develop a resilient mindset and adapt their strategies to maximize their financial outcomes.

Understanding the Role of Risk in Wealth Creation and Retirement Planning:

Risk plays a fundamental role in wealth creation and retirement planning. Without taking on some degree of risk, it becomes challenging to generate significant returns on investments or create substantial wealth over time. Risk allows for the possibility of higher rewards and can be a catalyst for financial growth.

In retirement planning, understanding risk is crucial for asset allocation and investment decisions. Different investment vehicles carry varying levels of risk, and it is important to strike a balance between risk and reward based on one's risk tolerance and financial goals. By understanding and managing risk effectively, individuals can position themselves for long-term financial success.

Overcoming the Fear of Failure and Embracing Calculated Risks:

The fear of failure often prevents individuals from taking necessary risks that can lead to financial growth. It is important to recognize that failure is an inherent part of any journey towards success. By reframing failure as an opportunity for learning and growth, individuals can overcome the fear associated with it.

Embracing calculated risks involves carefully assessing the potential rewards and potential downsides of an opportunity. It requires conducting thorough research, seeking expert advice when needed, and making informed decisions based on available information. Calculated risks are those that have been evaluated and align with one's risk tolerance and long-term financial objectives.

Learning from Setbacks and Adjusting Strategies Accordingly:

Setbacks and failures are valuable learning experiences that can inform future decisions and strategies. When setbacks occur, it is important to analyze the reasons behind them, identify lessons learned, and adjust strategies accordingly. By viewing setbacks as opportunities for improvement, individuals can refine their approaches and increase their chances of success.

Flexibility and adaptability are key when adjusting strategies based on setbacks. Recognizing that circumstances change and being open to refining plans allows for greater resilience and the ability to capitalize on new opportunities. Learning from failure and making necessary adjustments can lead to more effective wealth creation and retirement planning.

Embracing risk and learning from failure are integral components of wealth creation and retirement planning. By understanding the role of risk, overcoming the fear of failure, and embracing calculated risks, individuals can position themselves for long-term financial success. Furthermore, by learning from setbacks and adjusting strategies accordingly, individuals can adapt to changing circumstances and increase their chances of achieving their financial goals. Remember, embracing risk and learning from failure require a resilient mindset and a willingness to adapt. By cultivating these qualities, individuals can navigate the path towards wealth creation and a secure retirement.

Adopting a Growth Mindset

Adopting a growth mindset is essential for personal and financial growth, especially in the context of retirement planning. It involves embracing a mindset of continuous learning and personal growth, viewing challenges and setbacks as opportunities for improvement, and actively seeking new knowledge and staying updated on financial trends. This chapter explores the importance of adopting a growth mindset and its relevance to retirement planning. By cultivating a growth mindset, individuals can enhance their financial decision-making, adapt to changing circumstances, and maximize their potential for long-term success.

Embracing a Mindset of Continuous Learning and Personal Growth:

A growth mindset is characterized by a belief that abilities and intelligence can be developed through dedication and effort. In the context of retirement planning, adopting a growth mindset means recognizing that financial knowledge and skills can be acquired and improved upon over time. It involves a commitment to lifelong learning and personal growth, continuously seeking opportunities to expand one's financial literacy and expertise.

Embracing a mindset of continuous learning allows individuals to stay informed about new investment strategies, retirement planning options, and financial trends. It enables them to make more informed and effective decisions, adapt to changing market conditions, and seize opportunities that arise. By continuously expanding their knowledge, individuals can enhance their financial well-being and increase their chances of a successful retirement.

Viewing Challenges and Setbacks as Opportunities for Improvement:

A growth mindset involves viewing challenges and setbacks as opportunities for learning and improvement. Rather than being discouraged by obstacles, individuals with a growth mindset see them as stepping stones towards personal and financial growth. They recognize that setbacks provide valuable lessons and insights that can inform future decision-making.

In the context of retirement planning, setbacks such as market downturns or unexpected expenses can be viewed as opportunities to reassess financial strategies, identify areas for improvement, and adjust plans accordingly. By reframing challenges as learning experiences, individuals can become more resilient, develop creative problem-solving skills, and make more effective decisions to navigate their financial journey.

Seeking Out New Knowledge and Staying Updated on Financial Trends:

A growth mindset involves a proactive approach to seeking new knowledge and staying updated on financial trends. It requires individuals to actively engage in self-education, whether through reading books, attending seminars, participating in webinars, or seeking guidance from financial professionals. By staying informed, individuals can make informed decisions and capitalize on emerging opportunities.

Staying updated on financial trends allows individuals to anticipate changes in the investment landscape, identify potential risks and opportunities, and adjust their retirement plans accordingly. It enables them to make proactive adjustments to their investment portfolios, consider new retirement planning strategies, and stay ahead of the curve in an ever-changing financial landscape.

Adopting a growth mindset is essential for individuals seeking financial success and a fulfilling retirement. By embracing a mindset of continuous learning and personal growth, viewing challenges and setbacks as opportunities for improvement, and actively seeking new knowledge and staying updated on financial trends, individuals can enhance their financial decision-making, adapt to changing circumstances, and maximize their potential for long-term success. Remember, a growth mindset is a choice and a commitment to ongoing development. By cultivating this mindset, individuals can navigate their retirement journey with confidence and build a solid foundation for their financial future.

Cultivating Gratitude and Contentment

Practicing gratitude and being happy is important for a full and worthwhile life, especially when planning for retirement. It means being thankful for the present moment and the things you have, finding happiness in events and relationships instead of things, and avoiding the trap of letting your lifestyle get bigger and bigger. This chapter talks about how important it is to learn to be thankful and happy, and how that relates to saving for retirement. By embracing these traits, people can improve their health, lower their financial stress, and put real satisfaction ahead of excessive consumption.

Practicing Gratitude for the Present Moment and Your Resources:

To practice gratitude, you have to recognize and appreciate the present moment and the things you have. When planning for retirement, it's important to know the value of what you already have, whether it's a stable income, good health, helpful relationships, or a comfortable place to live. By focusing on the good things and showing thanks, people can feel like they have enough and are happy.

Gratitude helps people change their minds from constantly wanting more to realizing that what they already have is enough. People can feel less stressed about money and be happy with what they have now if they are aware of and grateful for what they already have. This change in how they think lets them make choices about their retirement goals and priorities that are more thoughtful and deliberate.

Finding Happiness in Experiences and Relationships:

When you retire, you can find happiness by putting more value on experiences and relationships than on things. It means valuing meaningful connections, doing things that bring joy and satisfaction, and focused on making experiences that people will remember. People can improve their general happiness and well-being by putting less emphasis on getting things and more on building experiences and relationships.

Finding happiness in events and relationships also makes people less dependent on too much consumption and the need to always get more stuff. It motivates people to spend their time, energy, and money on things that will make them truly happy and fulfilled. This change makes it possible to have a more balanced and meaningful retirement based on personal growth, making connections, and making moments that will last.

How to Avoid Lifestyle Inflation and Put True Fulfillment First:

Lifestyle inflation is the desire to spend more as income goes up. When planning for retirement, it's important not to give in to the pressure of social expectations and consumerism, which can lead to a higher standard of living and extra financial stress. Instead, people should focus on real happiness and make sure their spending is in line with their morals and passions.

By avoiding overconsumption and putting a higher value on real joy, people can put their money toward activities and investments that help them reach their retirement goals and give them lasting happiness. This could mean taking up a hobby, helping others, or spending money on activities that help with personal growth and well-being. People can live within their means, lower their financial burdens, and focus on what really matters in their retirement years if they learn to be content.

Practicing thanks and being happy is important for a happy retirement and a meaningful life. By being grateful for the present moment and the things you have, finding contentment in experiences and relationships, and avoiding the trap of lifestyle inflation, people can improve their health, reduce financial stress, and put true joy ahead of excessive consumption. Remember that true wealth isn't just about having things. It's also about how rich your experiences and relationships are. By practicing gratitude and being happy, people can make sure that their retirement is full of joy, meaning, and real satisfaction.

Seeking Financial Education and Mentorship

People who want to make smart financial choices and reach their retirement goals must get financial education and help from a mentor. It means knowing how important it is to learn about money, constantly looking for ways to learn more, finding mentors or advisors who can help and guide you, and being willing to learn from the experiences of others who have been financially successful. This chapter talks about why it's important to get financial education and a guide and how they affect planning for retirement. By doing these things, people can improve their financial knowledge, learn useful things, and feel confident about their financial journey.

Recognizing the Value of Financial Education:
Recognizing the value of financial education is the first step toward having a strong foundation for planning for

retirement. It means recognizing that you need to know and understand basic financial concepts in order to make good financial choices. By taking the time and making the effort to learn about money, people can get the skills they need to handle their finances well.

Financial education can be gained in a number of ways, such as by going to seminars, workshops, or online courses, reading books about personal finance and investment strategies, or using reliable financial tools and websites. By learning more about money, people can understand important ideas like budgeting, saving, retirement accounts, and tax planning better. This information gives them the power to make smart choices and take charge of their financial future.

Seeking teachers or Advisors:

Getting help from teachers or advisors who know a lot about money can be a huge help on the road to financial success. These people can give advice based on their own experiences and help you figure out how to plan for retirement. Mentors or advisors can give personalized advice, give different points of view on different investment choices, and help people come up with strategies that fit their own goals.

You can find mentors or advisors through professional networks, financial institutions, or organizations in your neighborhood. To build a relationship with a mentor or advisor, you need to talk to them regularly, share your financial goals and worries, and ask for their advice when making big financial choices. Their knowledge and unbiased view can help people avoid common mistakes, get the most out of their retirement plans, and stay on the right path to financial success.

Learning from the Experiences of Others:
Another important part of getting a financial education is being willing to learn from the experiences of people who have done well with money. Learning from people who have already been through the financial process can give you useful tips and lessons. Their experiences can give people ideas, tactics, and useful tips that they can use to plan for their own retirement.

People can learn from others in many ways, such as by reading the biographies or success stories of financially successful people, taking part in financial discussion forums or online communities, or going to networking events where they can meet people with similar goals. By listening to their stories, figuring out how they did things, and applying appropriate lessons to their own lives, people can get new ideas, learn more, and grow financially faster.

It's important for people who want to make smart financial choices and reach their retirement goals to get financial education and guidance. By understanding the importance of financial education, working with mentors or advisors, and being willing to learn from the experiences of others, people can improve their financial literacy, gain useful insights, and confidently move through their financial journey. Remember that learning about money and getting help with it is an ongoing process that takes a proactive mindset and a commitment to learning all the time. By doing these things, people can improve their financial knowledge and increase their chances of having a safe and happy retirement.

Nurturing a Positive Money Mindset

Nurturing a positive money mindset is crucial for financial well-being and successful retirement planning. It involves examining and challenging one's beliefs and attitudes towards money, cultivating a positive and healthy relationship with money, and celebrating financial victories. By embracing a positive money mindset, individuals can transform their financial outlook, make wiser financial decisions, and create a mindset of abundance and prosperity. This chapter explores the importance of nurturing a positive money mindset and its impact on retirement planning.

Examining and Challenging Beliefs and Attitudes Towards Money:

The first step in nurturing a positive money mindset is examining and challenging one's beliefs and attitudes towards money. It involves becoming aware of any negative or limiting beliefs that may hinder financial growth and replacing them with more empowering beliefs. Common negative beliefs include "money is evil" or "I'll never be wealthy."

By questioning these beliefs and challenging their validity, individuals can reframe their mindset to see money as a tool for creating opportunities, supporting their goals, and making a positive impact. This shift in perspective allows individuals to approach their finances with optimism, openness, and a willingness to learn.

Cultivating a Positive and Healthy Relationship with Money:
Cultivating a positive and healthy relationship with money involves treating money with respect, gratitude, and mindfulness. It means recognizing that money is a resource that can be

managed wisely to support one's goals and values. Developing a healthy relationship with money involves avoiding extremes such as excessive materialism or deprivation, and instead finding a balance that aligns with personal values and financial goals.

Practicing gratitude for the financial resources one has, regardless of the amount, can help cultivate a positive money mindset. Appreciating the opportunities money provides and being mindful of spending habits fosters a sense of abundance and contentment. By nurturing a positive relationship with money, individuals can make financial decisions from a place of confidence, self-worth, and alignment with their values.

Celebrating Financial Victories and Embracing Abundance:

Celebrating financial victories, no matter how small, is an important aspect of nurturing a positive money mindset. Acknowledging progress and accomplishments reinforces positive financial behaviors and reinforces the belief in one's ability to achieve financial goals. It can involve celebrating milestones such as paying off debt, reaching savings targets, or successfully investing.

Embracing a mindset of abundance and prosperity involves recognizing that there are limitless possibilities for financial growth and success. It means shifting from a mindset of scarcity to one of abundance, where individuals believe that there is enough for everyone and that opportunities for financial well-being are abundant. This mindset encourages individuals to seek and create new opportunities, be open to abundance, and approach retirement planning with optimism and confidence.

Nurturing a positive money mindset is essential for successful retirement planning and overall financial well-being.

By examining and challenging beliefs and attitudes towards money, cultivating a positive and healthy relationship with money, and celebrating financial victories, individuals can transform their financial outlook and approach retirement planning with optimism and abundance. Remember, a positive money mindset is a continuous practice that requires self-awareness, mindfulness, and intentional effort. By nurturing a positive money mindset, individuals can pave the way for a financially secure and fulfilling retirement.

By embracing the mindset of financial freedom, you are laying the foundation for a successful retirement. In the next chapter, we will explore how to unleash your true potential and leverage your unique skills and passions to create a retirement plan that aligns with your goals and aspirations.

Continue reading in Chapter 3: Unleashing Your True Potential.

4

Unleashing Your True Potential

In Chapter 3, we delve into the importance of unleashing your true potential and leveraging your unique skills and passions to create a retirement plan that aligns with your goals and aspirations. Let's explore the key elements of discovering and utilizing your true potential in retirement.

Self-Reflection and Personal Assessment

Engaging in self-reflection and personal assessment is a crucial step in preparing for a successful retirement journey. It involves introspection to identify one's strengths, interests, and values, assessing the skills and experiences gained throughout one's career, and identifying areas for growth and development. By undertaking this self-assessment, individuals can gain clarity about their personal aspirations, align their retirement plans with their values, and make informed decisions that lead to a fulfilling and purpose-driven retirement. This chapter explores the importance of self-reflection and personal assessment in retirement preparation.

Engaging in Self-Reflection:

Self-reflection is an introspective process that allows individuals to gain a deeper understanding of themselves, their desires, and their priorities. In the context of retirement planning, self-reflection is crucial for identifying personal strengths, interests, and values that can shape the retirement journey. By reflecting on what brings joy, fulfillment, and meaning, individuals can align their retirement plans with their true selves.

Self-reflection involves asking meaningful questions such as "What are my passions and interests?", "What are my core values?", and "What activities bring me the greatest sense of fulfillment?" By honestly exploring these questions, individuals can gain insights into their unique strengths and desires, which can guide their retirement planning and help them make choices that are in line with their authentic selves.

Assessing Skills and Experiences:

Assessing the skills and experiences gained throughout one's career is another crucial aspect of personal assessment for retirement planning. Individuals can reflect on their professional achievements, the skills they have developed, and the experiences they have acquired over the course of their working life. This assessment allows individuals to identify transferable skills that can be leveraged in retirement, as well as areas where further development may be beneficial.

By assessing their skills and experiences, individuals can determine how their existing knowledge and expertise can be applied in retirement, whether it is through starting a new venture, engaging in volunteer work, or pursuing a passion project. This assessment also helps individuals recognize areas where additional learning or skill enhancement may be required to support their retirement goals.

Identifying Areas for Growth and Development:

In the process of self-assessment, it is important to identify areas for growth and development as part of retirement preparation. Retirement offers an opportunity for personal growth and learning, and individuals should consider areas where they would like to expand their knowledge or develop new skills. This could involve exploring new hobbies, acquiring financial literacy, or investing in personal development activities.

Identifying areas for growth and development allows individuals to proactively plan for their retirement journey. By setting goals for self-improvement, individuals can stay engaged, maintain a sense of purpose, and continue to learn and grow during retirement. This self-directed growth ensures that retirement becomes a period of exploration, discovery, and ongoing personal development.

Engaging in self-reflection and personal assessment is a vital step in retirement preparation. By engaging in self-reflection, individuals can identify their strengths, interests, and values that will guide their retirement plans. Assessing skills and experiences allows individuals to leverage their expertise and determine areas for further development. By identifying areas for growth and development, individuals can proactively plan for a fulfilling retirement journey.

Remember, self-reflection and personal assessment are ongoing processes that should be revisited and adapted as individuals move through different stages of retirement. By embracing self-reflection and personal assessment, individuals can embark on a retirement journey that aligns with their true selves and leads to a purposeful and rewarding retirement.

Discovering Your Passions and Purpose

Finding your passions and meaning is a life-changing process that has a big impact on how fulfilling your retirement will be. It means discovering your interests, hobbies, and activities that make you happy, finding purpose and meaning by making sure your activities are in line with your values, and finding new interests and ways to grow as a person. By going on this journey of self-discovery, people can make their retirement years full of satisfaction, meaning, and personal growth. This chapter talks about how important it is to find interests and a purpose after you retire.

Learning More About Your Interests, Hobbies, and Activities:
When you retire, you can do things that make you happy and give you a sense of satisfaction. It is a time to try new things and find out what you like to do. Take the time to think about things that have always interested you or given you a deep sense of pleasure. Whether it's painting, gardening, playing an instrument, or doing things outside, these hobbies can give you a useful retirement.

Exploration can include trying out new hobbies or going back to ones you didn't have time to do fully when you were working. By spending time on these interests, people can feel joy, creativity, and personal happiness all over again.

Doing things that make you feel like your true self gives your retirement journey a sense of meaning and fulfillment.

Finding Purpose and Meaning:
When you retire, you have the chance to align your activities with your values and find greater meaning in the things you do every day. Think about what it really means to you and how you can make the world a better place. It could mean doing volunteer work, being a mentor to other people, or doing things that help issues you care about.

By doing things that are in line with your values, you can give your retirement a sense of purpose and meaning. When you live in a way that is in line with what is most important to you, you feel fulfilled and happy. Finding your purpose in retirement means getting in touch with your core values, figuring out where you can make a difference, and doing things that are in line with your sense of purpose.

Finding New Interests and Opportunities:
Retirement is a good time to try out new things and find new ways to grow as a person. As you start this journey of learning, keep an open mind and a sense of wonder. Look for new things to do, try new things, and get out of your comfort zone.

Be willing to learn and explore new things. Sign up for classes or workshops that will teach you new things or skills. Go to new places and learn about different ways of life. Join different groups and make friends with people who like the same things you do.

Finding new interests and opportunities not only helps you grow as a person but also improves your general health. It keeps your mind busy, sparks your creativity, and gives your retirement years a feeling of excitement and adventure.

Finding your passions and your meaning is an important part of having a happy retirement. By figuring out what you're passionate about, making sure your activities are in line with your values, and finding new hobbies and opportunities, you can create a retirement that is full of life, has a purpose, and gives you a deep sense of satisfaction. Remember that this is an ongoing journey of self-discovery. Embrace the process with a sense of wonder, an open mind, and a desire to discover new things. By figuring out what you're passionate about and what you want to do with your life, you can make sure your retirement is full of joy, meaning, and personal growth.

Capitalizing on Transferable Skills

When you're getting ready to retire, it's a good idea to use the skills you've gained throughout your work. Transferable skills are skills and information that can be used in different fields, roles, and situations. People can use their professional experience to create a meaningful and purposeful retirement by recognizing the value of their skills, figuring out how they can be used in new and fulfilling ways during retirement, and looking into opportunities for mentoring or consulting based on their expertise. This chapter talks about how important it is to use transferable skills after you leave.

Seeing the Value of Transferable Skills:

Transferable skills, like the ability to communicate, lead, solve problems, and handle projects, are often learned on the job. These skills are useful in more than one job or field, and they can be used in different situations. Recognizing the value of these skills is important when planning for retirement because it lets people use their expertise in new ways and make valuable contributions.

Transferable skills are those that a person has worked on and improved over the course of their job. They show that they know a lot of different things, can change, and can keep learning. By recognizing the importance of these skills, people can look forward to retirement with confidence and understand the unique contributions they can make based on their work experience.

Finding New and Fulfilling Ways to Use Transferable Skills:

Retirement is a chance to use transferable skills in new and satisfying ways. It means figuring out how to use these skills to follow personal interests, take part in meaningful activities, or help the community. For example, strong leadership skills learned at work can be used in mentorship jobs, where people help and guide others in their personal and professional growth.

Skills that can be used in different situations can also be used to start a small business or a coaching practice. People can use their knowledge to help others by giving them useful services or solutions. People can have a fulfilling, purposeful, and mentally stimulating retirement by combining their interests or passions with skills that can be used elsewhere.

Exploring Opportunities for Mentoring or Consulting:

When you retire, you can look into jobs as a mentor or consultant based on what you know. Mentoring is a way for people to help and guide others by sharing their knowledge and experiences. This can be done through business networks, community groups, or schools. Mentoring gives people a sense of satisfaction and lets them make a difference in the lives of others.

Consulting is another way to use transferable skills to make money. Many groups and people look to retired professionals for advice and ideas on how to deal with difficult problems. Consulting lets people keep up with their professional networks, keep their minds active, and work on projects that match their hobbies and skills.

Using transferable skills to your advantage is a good way to plan for retirement. People can use their professional experience to create a meaningful and rewarding retirement by recognizing the value of their skills, finding ways to use them in new and satisfying ways, and looking into opportunities for mentoring or consulting. Transferable skills are the basis for continuing to learn, be active, and help others after retirement. Take advantage of the chances that come up because of these skills, and let them lead you to a retirement that shows your knowledge, love, and desire to make a difference in the world.

Pursuing Lifelong Learning

Pursuing ongoing learning is a way of thinking that can change your life. It can help you grow as a person, keep your mind active, and feel like you've accomplished something. When you quit, it's even more important to keep learning because it gives you chances to learn new things, try out new things you're interested in, and keep your mind sharp. This article talks about how important it is to keep learning throughout your life, the different ways you can do that, and the benefits it brings to people as they move toward retirement.

Adopting a mindset of continuous learning:

Adopting a mindset of continuous learning is a strong way to help yourself grow and improve. It means going through life with a sense of wonder, a hunger for knowledge, and a willingness to try out new ideas and points of view. People in retirement can keep their minds active, engaged, and open to new situations if they think this way.

Continuous learning keeps people's minds sharp and feeds their intellectual interest. It lets people learn about many different things, encourages critical thought, and grows a love of learning that will last a lifetime. By adopting this way of thinking, retirees can reach their full potential, find new interests, and continue to grow as people.

Exploring Educational Options:

Retirement is a great time to look into educational options that can help you learn new things and improve your skills. There are many things to think about, such as taking classes at a local community college or university, going to workshops or seminars, or using online learning tools.

Community schools and universities often have classes for retirees and other adults who want to learn something new. These classes cover a wide range of topics, so people can learn more about things that interest them or gain new skills.

Workshops and seminars give retirees the chance to learn about specific topics in depth. This helps them become experts in a certain area.

Online learning platforms have changed the way people learn for the rest of their lives by giving them access to a wide range of classes from well-known institutions and experts. People can learn at their own pace and in a place and time that is convenient for them by using these tools. Online classes cover a wide range of topics, from history and literature to technology and science, and offer an interactive way to learn.

Engaging in Intellectual Pursuits:
Engaging in intellectual pursuits is a key part of ongoing learning in retirement. It means constantly looking for things to do that make you think and help you get smarter. To participate in intellectual activities, you can read books, join book clubs, take part in discussion groups, or go to lectures and conferences.

The more you read, the more you learn and the more interesting discussions you can have. Book clubs give people a chance to talk to each other and talk about books, which helps build a sense of community and shared learning. Discussion groups and classes give retirees the chance to talk about things that make them think and keep up with current topics and trends.

Intellectual activities not only keep the mind sharp, but they also give a sense of satisfaction and a way to connect with people who like the same things you do. They give us chances to try out new ideas, test our theories, and learn more about the world.

Continuing to learn after retirement is a great way to grow as a person, keep your mind active, and live a full life. By having the attitude of always learning, looking for educational opportunities, and doing intellectual things, retirees can keep learning new things, finding new interests, and keeping their minds sharp. Learning is something you do for the rest of your life, and retirement is a great time to focus on intellectual activities. Embrace the joy of learning, feed your curiosity, and let the pursuit of knowledge lead you to a retirement full of growth, discovery, and satisfaction.

Embracing Entrepreneurship

Entrepreneurship is a great way to follow your interests, make money, and find fulfillment in your later years. It means thinking about entrepreneurship as a way to use your skills and hobbies to make money, finding business opportunities that match your skills, and learning how to start and run a small business. This chapter talks about how important it is to be an entrepreneur in retirement, how to find good business chances, and how important it is to know the basics of entrepreneurship.

Entrepreneurship as a Possible Path:
  Retirement is a great time to think about entrepreneurship as a possible path. It lets people turn their interests and hobbies into money-making businesses. By starting their own business,

retirees can make something that fits their hobbies, gives them a sense of purpose, and gives them the freedom to work on their own terms.

Entrepreneurship lets you set your own schedule, make your own choices, and work on projects that interest and excite you. It gives retirees the chance to use their years of experience, skills, and business knowledge to make money and add value to the market.

Finding Business Opportunities:

One of the most important steps in becoming an entrepreneur in retirement is to find the right business opportunity. Start by thinking about your interests, hobbies, and skills. Think about the market's needs and wants as well as the people who would be interested in your business idea.

Entrepreneurs who are retired often do well by focusing on niche markets or offering specialized services. For example, if you love gardening, you could start a business that helps people with their planting or gardening. If you know a lot about a certain field, you could offer coaching services to businesses or people who want help in that field.

It is important to study the market, look at the competition, and make a clear business plan that explains your value proposition, target market, marketing strategies, and financial projections. This process helps you improve your business idea and makes it more likely to work.

Learning the Basics of Entrepreneurship:

Before starting out as an entrepreneur, it is important to learn the basics of how to start and run a small business. This means knowing the law, how to handle money, marketing tactics, and how to get new customers.

Think about going to workshops, seminars, or online training that teach you how to start and run a small business. Local business development centers and entrepreneurship programs often help people who want to start their own business by giving them tools and putting them in touch with mentors.

By getting the skills and knowledge you need, you can deal with the challenges of being an entrepreneur better, make better choices, and increase the chances of building a successful business.

When you start your own business after retirement, it can lead to new chances, personal fulfillment, and financial freedom. Retirees can start a rewarding entrepreneurial journey by looking at entrepreneurship as a path, finding business chances that fit with their interests and skills, and learning about the basics of entrepreneurship. Entrepreneurship gives people the chance to make money, change the world for the better, and stay busy and have a reason after they retire. Embrace the spirit of entrepreneurship, work on your ideas, and let your interests lead you to a satisfying and successful business you can start when you retire.

Emphasizing Social Impact and Volunteerism

Focusing on social impact and volunteering in retirement is a meaningful way to give back to the community, make a positive difference in the lives of others, and find a sense of purpose and satisfaction. It means looking for ways to make a difference in the world, doing volunteer work, and using your skills and experiences to help causes that fit with your values. This chapter talks about why it's important to focus on social effect and volunteering in retirement, what it can do for people and communities, and how to get involved.

Exploring Social Impact Opportunities:
Retirement is a great time to look into social impact opportunities and help issues that are important to you. Start by thinking about social problems or interests where you can make a real difference. These can include saving the earth, educating people, helping people get out of poverty, and taking care of their health.

Find out about area nonprofits, community groups, or projects that work on these problems. Most of the time, these groups need help from people to run their programs and projects. Also, think about joining networks or platforms that connect retired people with service opportunities. This will help you find projects that match your skills and interests.

Volunteering:
Volunteering is a great way to give back to your community

and make a good difference. It gives you a chance to meet people with similar interests, build important relationships, and help other people. Volunteering gives you the chance to make a real difference in the lives of people and towns, whether you help out at a local shelter, teach children, or help clean up the environment.

Think about the skills and experiences you've gained over the course of your life and work. Look for service positions where you can use your skills to make a bigger difference. For example, if you have a background in business, you could help nonprofits manage their money or come up with ways to keep getting money in the long run.

Using Skills and Experiences:
Retirees have a lot of skills, knowledge, and experiences that they have gained over the course of their lives. Using these tools well can make a big difference in social impact efforts. Find out how you can use your skills and experiences to help other people.

Think about training programs or other projects that help and guide people who need it. Offer workshops, training events, or consultations to nonprofits or community groups to share your knowledge. By using your unique set of skills, you can give other people more power and help them reach their goals.

Benefits of Putting an emphasis on social impact and volunteering:
There are many benefits to putting an emphasis on social impact and volunteering in retirement. It gives you a feeling of

purpose, satisfaction, and a new sense of your own worth. Volunteering helps people make new friends and feel like they belong in their neighborhood. Studies have shown that volunteering is good for your general health and happiness and makes you feel better physically and mentally.

Also, if retirees do good things, they can leave a lasting memory and make the future better for future generations. Their work can encourage others to get active and make a difference for the better in the world.

Social impact and volunteering are great ways to give back, make a difference, and find satisfaction in retirement. By looking for ways to make a difference in the world, doing charity work, and using their skills and experiences, retirees can help causes they care about and improve the lives of others. Take advantage of the chance to make a real difference, make new friends, and leave a lasting mark on the world through acts of love and kindness. Together, we can make the world a more caring and welcoming place for everyone.

Balancing Leisure and Productivity

In retirement, it's important to find a good mix between fun and useful things to do. It means setting aside time to relax, take care of yourself, and do other fun things while also doing things that have a reason and make you feel good about yourself. This chapter talks about how important it is to find a balance between having fun and getting things done when you're retired, what benefits that has for your general well-being, and how to find that balance.

Allocating Time for rest and Leisure:
Retirement is a great time to put rest and leisure at the top of your list. After years of hard work, it's important to take time to relax and recharge. Do things that make you happy and help you relax, like reading, learning a hobby, spending time with people you care about, or taking in nature.

Set up a plan that gives you time to relax on a regular basis. Set aside times during the day or week to do things you enjoy without feeling guilty or pressured. By putting aside time for fun, you can boost your energy, lower your stress, and improve your general health.

Exploring and Pursuing Hobbies:
When you retire, you have time to explore and pursue hobbies you may not have had time for when you were working. Do things that make you happy and fulfilled, like learning to play an instrument, drawing, gardening, or traveling.

Find the leisure activities that you really enjoy and that fit with your ideals and passions. Give yourself time to grow and develop these hobbies, which will make your retirement more enjoyable. Leisure activities are not only fun, but they also help people grow, be creative, and feel like they can express themselves.

Engaging in Activities with a Purpose:
Leisure and relaxation are important in retirement, but

so is keeping a feeling of purpose and being productive. Participating in activities with a purpose that give you a sense of accomplishment and fulfillment is good for your general health.

You might want to do things that match your skills, hobbies, and values. This can be done by doing things like volunteering, teaching, starting a small business, or working part-time. With these kinds of activities, you can help others, make a good difference, and keep a sense of purpose and fulfillment.

Finding mix: In retirement, it takes effort and self-awareness to find a good mix between leisure and work. Think about what you want, what you need, and what your goals are. Think about how much time you want to spend on fun things versus useful things.

Make a schedule that includes both fun and useful things to do so that you can rest and get things done at the same time. Set reasonable goals for each day, week, or month to feel like you're making progress and staying on track. Remember that the goal isn't to stay busy all the time, but to find happiness through a well-rounded retirement.

Finding a good balance between free time and work is important for general happiness and a fulfilling retirement. Retirees can find a healthy balance that improves their physical, mental, and emotional well-being by setting aside time for relaxation and leisure, pursuing leisure interests, and taking part in meaningful activities. Embrace the freedom of retirement by finding joy in things you do for fun and satisfaction in things you do for a reason. This will make your retirement both relaxing and productive.

Embracing New Opportunities and Embracing Change

Embracing new opportunities and change is crucial in retirement as it opens doors to personal and professional growth, allows for the exploration of new possibilities, and facilitates the development of a fulfilling retirement journey. This chapter highlights the significance of remaining open to new opportunities, seizing growth prospects, and adapting to new roles and identities in retirement with enthusiasm and optimism.

Remaining Open to New Possibilities:

Retirement is a phase of life that offers the freedom to explore new possibilities and embark on fresh ventures. It is important to maintain an open mind and embrace the potential for change. Instead of clinging to familiar routines, be receptive to new experiences, ideas, and opportunities that come your way.

Stay curious and engage in activities that challenge you intellectually, emotionally, or physically. Explore different hobbies, take on new projects, or venture into unfamiliar territories. By remaining open to new possibilities, you can discover hidden talents, passions, and areas of interest that may have remained untapped during your previous career.

Seizing Opportunities for Personal and Professional Growth:

Retirement presents an ideal time for personal and professional growth. Seize opportunities to expand your knowledge, acquire new skills, and engage in meaningful endeavors. Take advantage of educational programs, workshops, or online courses that align with your interests and aspirations.

Consider pursuing part-time work, consulting, or mentoring opportunities that allow you to share your expertise and contribute to the community. Embrace the chance to develop new skills or build on existing ones. By continuously investing in your personal and professional growth, you can maintain a sense of purpose, keep your mind sharp, and enhance your overall satisfaction in retirement.

Adapting to New Roles and Identities:

Retirement often involves a shift in roles and identities. Embrace this transition with enthusiasm and optimism, recognizing it as an opportunity for personal reinvention. Embrace the idea that retirement is not the end of your journey but a new chapter waiting to be written.

Take the time to reflect on who you are and who you want to become in retirement. Identify the values, passions, and aspirations that define your new identity. Embrace new roles such as being a grandparent, a volunteer, a mentor, or an entrepreneur. Embrace the chance to redefine yourself and create a retirement lifestyle that aligns with your true self.

Embracing new opportunities and change in retirement is essential for personal growth, fulfillment, and a vibrant retirement experience. By remaining open to new possibilities, seizing growth opportunities, and adapting to new roles and identities, retirees can embark on a journey of continued self-discovery and meaningful engagement with the world around them. Embrace the freedom and flexibility that retirement offers, and approach each day with enthusiasm, curiosity, and optimism. Embrace the unknown with open arms, and let it guide you towards new adventures and a fulfilling retirement journey.

By unleashing your true potential, you will discover a world of possibilities and fulfillment in your retirement. In the next chapter, we will explore innovative income generation strategies that go beyond traditional employment.

Get ready to explore new avenues of financial independence in Chapter 4: Income Generation Strategies.

5

Income Generation Strategies

In Chapter 4, we dive into innovative income generation strategies that go beyond traditional employment. Retirement is no longer solely about relying on a pension or Social Security. Let's explore various avenues to create multiple streams of income and achieve true financial independence in retirement.

The Power of Passive Income

Passive income has a lot of promise in retirement because it can provide a steady stream of income without requiring constant work. This article looks at what passive income is, how it can help people in retirement, and the different ways it can be made, such as through rental properties, dividends, and royalties. Also, it goes into detail about how to make passive income through investing and owning assets.

Understanding Passive Income:

Passive income is money that comes from sources that don't take much effort or time on a regular basis. Passive income is different from active income, which involves trading time for money. It lets people make money while enjoying the freedom and ease of retirement. This kind of income gives you financial security, makes you less reliant on standard retirement savings, and opens up new opportunities.

Exploring Sources of Passive Income:

There are many sources of passive income that can be looked into after retirement. Having rental homes gives you the chance to make regular rental income. By buying real estate and renting it out, retirees can get a steady flow of cash without having to do much day-to-day work.

Stock dividends and investments in companies that pay dividends can also be a source of idle income. Dividends are a part of a company's profits that are given to its shareholders. This is how retirees can make money from their investment accounts without having to actively manage them.

Royalties from intellectual property, such as books, songs, or patents, can also be a good way to make money without doing anything. When these assets are licensed or sold, royalties are made. This is a steady source of income.

Passive income can be made through investments and owning assets. Investments are a key part of making passive income in retirement. Retirees can get regular gains on their investments by putting their money in income-generating assets like stocks, bonds, mutual funds, and real estate investment trusts (REITs).

Passive income can also come from having assets, like rental properties or a business. By putting together a collection of assets that bring in money, retirees can create a steady source of income that requires little work on their part.

Also, spreading out your investments and using a long-term investment plan can help you get the most out of your passive income. By investing in different types of assets and using a "buy and hold" strategy, seniors can reduce risks and get the most out of their investments as they grow over time.

Passive income is very important in retirement because it gives you financial security, independence, and the freedom to live a happy life after you retire. By knowing what passive income is and looking into different sources like rental properties, dividends, and royalties, retirees can find ways to make money without having to work all the time.

Through investments and owning assets, retirees can build a steady flow of income that supports the lifestyle they want in retirement. Accept the power of passive income and let it help you have a happy and successful retirement.

Real Estate Ventures

Real estate investments offer good chances to make money from rent, which makes it an attractive way to invest in retirement. This chapter talks about the potential for rental income from real estate investments. It also talks about the basics of real estate investing, such as how to choose a property and how to manage it. Finally, it talks about other options, such as real estate investment trusts (REITs), for people who want to diversify their investment portfolios.

Exploring Real Estate Investment Options for Rental Income:
When you invest in real estate for rental income, you buy properties with the goal of renting them out to renters and getting regular rent payments. This approach has a number of benefits, such as a steady cash flow, possible tax benefits, and the chance that the property will go up in value over time.

Investors can think about single-family homes, condos, and apartment buildings with multiple units as possible rental income sources. These homes can be rented out to people or families who need a place to live, giving you a steady stream of renting income.

Commercial sites like offices, stores, and industrial buildings can also be rented out to make money. These properties are used by businesses and groups, and renting them out can be a stable and long-term way to make money.

Basics of Real Estate Investing:

To be successful in real estate investing, you need to think carefully about many things. It's important to choose the right property, and things like location, market demand, rental prospects, and property condition should be carefully looked at. Investing in places with a high demand for rentals, closeness to amenities, and growth prospects can help you get the most out of your rental income.

For real estate businesses to be successful, they need to have good property management. This includes things like finding good tenants, collecting rent, taking care of the property, and quickly responding to tenant complaints. Hiring a professional property management company can help make things run more smoothly and make sure rental properties are managed well.

Alternative Real Estate Investment Options:

Real estate investment trusts (REITs) can be a good choice for retirees who want to broaden their investment portfolios or who want to invest in real estate without having to do much of the work themselves. REITs are ways for multiple investors to pool their money to buy and run properties that bring in money. Investors can buy shares in publicly traded REITs, which give them access to real estate assets and the chance of rental income without having to own or run the properties themselves.

Investors have more options with REITs because they can buy and sell shares on stock markets. Also, REITs often give a big chunk of their earnings to owners as dividends, which makes them a good way to make passive income in retirement.

Real estate investments are a great way to make money in retirement through rental income. By looking into real estate investment choices, choosing properties wisely, and managing rental properties well, retirees can get a steady flow of cash and possibly see their property value rise. REITs are a good choice for people who want to diversify their investments and make money while they sleep. Real estate investments can be a valuable part of a well-rounded investment portfolio and help you have a financially safe and fulfilling retirement, whether you own the property directly or invest in REITs.

Online Business and E-Commerce

The internet has changed the way companies work, giving retirees exciting opportunities to start their own online businesses after they retire. This chapter looks at how the power of the internet could be used to start an online business. It looks at e-commerce sites, dropshipping, and affiliate marketing as possible business models. Also, it shows how important it is to find niche markets and build a strong online profile if you want to be successful.

Using the Power of the Internet:
When people retire, they can take advantage of the internet's global reach and ease of use by starting an online business. Online businesses have the advantage of low costs to start up, freedom in how they run, and the possibility of growing

indefinitely.

E-Commerce Platforms:
E-commerce platforms are the backbone of online businesses. They offer a digital marketplace where goods or services can be shown and sold. Platforms like Shopify, WooCommerce, and BigCommerce have easy-to-use interfaces, customizable stores, and built-in payment gateways that make it easier for retirees to get online.

Dropshipping is a way to run a business that gets rid of the need to keep track of inventory and process orders. Suppliers can help retirees by taking care of supplies and shipping, so the retirees can focus on marketing and customer service. This plan makes it easier to start an online business in retirement because it requires less money up front and is easier to run.

Affiliate marketing is when you promote the goods or services of another company and get a cut of each sale made through your referral links. Retirees can use their knowledge and interests to create content, build an audience, and suggest relevant goods or services through their website or social media channels. This model lets retirees make money by making sure their suggestions are right for their niche group.

Finding narrow Markets:
It's important for an online business to find and focus on narrow markets. By focusing on specific interests, passions, or underserved customer segments, retirees can set themselves apart from bigger competitors and build a loyal customer

base. To find a profitable niche market, you need to do market study, find out what consumers want, and know what your competitors are doing.

Creating a Strong Online Presence:
If you want to draw customers and build credibility, you need to have a strong online presence. Retirees can build a professional website or blog, make it easy for search engines to find, and connect with their target audience through social media. Creating useful content, using good branding strategies, and using search engine optimization can help bring in more traffic and make an online business more visible.

The internet has given retirees a lot of options for starting their own online businesses after they quit. Retirees can take advantage of the potential of the digital world by using e-commerce platforms, looking into dropshipping and partner marketing, finding niche markets, and building a strong online presence. By starting an online business, seniors can follow their interests, make money, and enjoy the freedom and satisfaction of being their own boss. Use the power of online business and e-commerce to make your retirement more interesting.

Creating and Monetizing Intellectual Property

People can use their knowledge, skills, and creativity to build intellectual property and make money from it after they retire. This chapter looks at the different ways to create intellectual property and make money from it, like writing books, making online classes, or making software. It goes into detail about the steps needed to bring ideas to market and make money from them. It also shows how important digital platforms and good marketing strategies are for reaching a wider audience.

Exploring Opportunities to Make and Sell Intellectual Property:

Retirees have a lot of information and experience that can be turned into valuable intellectual property. You could try writing books, making online courses, making software or apps, or even coming up with new goods. These kinds of intellectual property could bring in money and have a long-lasting effect.

Steps to Get Ideas on the Market and Make Money:

There are a few key steps to getting intellectual property on the market. First, you need to do a lot of study to find out who your target audience is, what the market needs, and how your competitors are doing. This helps to shape ideas and make sure they make sense to the audience in mind. Next, the process of making something starts. This could be writing a book, making an online lesson, or making software. To stand out in a busy market, you need to pay close attention to details, make sure your product is of high quality, and make it your own.

Once the creation is done, it's important to protect intellectual property rights with copyrights, trademarks, or patents, based on what the creation is. This keeps people from using it without permission and lets the right money be made. Pricing strategies should be carefully thought out to make sure they accurately show the value of the intellectual property.

Using Digital Platforms and Marketing Strategies:
   Digital platforms give artists the chance to reach a larger audience in ways that have never been possible before. Authors can self-publish e-books through platforms like Amazon Kindle Direct Publishing, and online course creators can use platforms like Udemy or Teachable to share their work. App stores and internet marketplaces are two ways for software developers to sell their work.

To get the most out of intellectual property, it's important to have good marketing tactics. This includes making websites, blogs, and social media tools that get people interested online. Using techniques like content marketing, email marketing, and search engine optimization (SEO), the target group can be attracted and kept interested. Collaborations, partnerships, and marketing through people who have a lot of impact can also help spread intellectual property.

When people retire, they have a unique chance to use their imagination and skills to make and sell intellectual property. Retirees can use their knowledge to make money and leave a long-lasting effect by writing books, making online courses, or making software. By taking the steps needed to bring ideas to market, protecting intellectual property rights, and using digital platforms and successful marketing strategies, retirees can reach a wider audience and use their creations to their fullest potential. Embrace the process of making intellectual property and making money from it, and see how your ideas can change the world.

Freelancing and Consulting

People can use their professional skills to their advantage after they retire by doing freelance work or consulting in their areas. This chapter looks at the possibility of using one's skills and experience to offer freelance services or advice. It also looks at how to find a market need, use networks to your advantage, start a freelance business, and market services well.

Using Professional Expertise:
People who have retired have a lot of knowledge and experience that they have gained during their jobs. By doing freelance work or consulting, retirees can use their experience to help companies or people in need with valuable insights, advice, and solutions. This lets them keep making important contributions in their field while having the freedom of working for themselves.

Finding Out What the Market Wants:

Before you start freelancing or coaching, you need to find out what the market wants from your skills and services. Researching industry trends, analyzing market wants, and finding market gaps can help you figure out if your products or services will work. You can also position yourself effectively by thinking about your target audience, your competition, and the needs of potential clients.

Using Your Network:

Retirees have the benefit of having built up a large network of professional contacts over the course of their jobs. Using these links to your advantage can lead to good opportunities and referrals. You can meet possible clients, partners, and mentors at networking events, industry conferences, and on online platforms like LinkedIn. Building and maintaining connections with people in your field can help you get freelance work or consulting gigs.

Setting up a Freelance Business:

Retirees who want to start a successful freelance business need to think about important things like law requirements, money management, and branding. Registering as a freelancer or single proprietor, getting any licenses or permits you need, and opening a separate bank account for business transactions will make sure that you are following the rules and that your finances are clear. Having a professional website, portfolio, and business cards, as well as a strong brand personality, gives your services more credibility.

Effectively marketing your services is a must if you want to get clients and build a strong freelance profile. A strong way to get people interested in you is to make an interesting online portfolio or website that shows off your skills, experience, and past successes. Using digital marketing tactics like search engine optimization (SEO), content marketing, and social media can help you be seen and reach more people. By asking for testimonials, referrals, and recommendations from your network, you can improve your image and bring in new clients.

Freelancing and advising are ways for retired people to keep using their professional skills and make a positive difference in their field. By figuring out what the market needs, using their networks, starting a freelance business, and using good marketing techniques, retirees can become in-demand freelancers or advisors. By choosing this flexible and independent job path, retirees can keep working in their field and enjoy the benefits of being their own boss. Use your professional skills, start freelancing or consulting, and enjoy the success and satisfaction that come with using your skills after you leave.

Investment Strategies for Retirement

Investment plans are a key part of making sure you can retire with enough money. This chapter talks about why it's important to have a diversified portfolio of investments, what those choices are, and the basic ideas behind asset allocation, risk management, and long-term wealth accumulation.

Diversifying Your Investment Portfolio:

Diversifying your investments is a key way to reduce risk and get the most out of your money in retirement. By spreading their investments across different asset classes, such as stocks, bonds, mutual funds, and exchange-traded funds (ETFs), retirees can lower their exposure to the volatility of any one investment. Diversification makes it possible to make money from many different sources and helps protect against losses.

Exploring Investment Options:

Retirees can choose from a number of ways to put their money to work. Stocks have the chance to go up in value and pay dividends, while bonds offer a steady income and security. Mutual funds and exchange-traded funds (ETFs) offer diversified investing portfolios that are managed by experts and give you access to a wide range of assets. Real estate investment trusts (REITs) are a way to invest in real estate without actually owning the land. Each choice has its own risks and possible rewards, so retirees should think carefully about their financial goals and how much risk they are willing to take before making a choice.

Understanding Asset Allocation and Risk Management:

Asset allocation is the process of dividing investments into different asset groups based on risk tolerance, time horizon, and financial goals. By putting their money in different kinds of investments, retirees can find a good mix between risk and possible returns. Risk management is the process of figuring out how to deal with the risks that come with each business, such as changes in the market, inflation, and interest rates. Diversifying your investments, adjusting your portfolio on a regular basis, and keeping up with market trends are all important parts of managing risk well.

Long-Term Wealth Accumulation:
Saving for retirement takes a long time, and focusing on long-term growth is important for building wealth. Retirees should be disciplined and not give in to the desire to trade on short-term market changes. By putting money into retirement accounts like IRAs and 401(k)s on a regular basis, you can use the power of compounding over time. Reinvesting earnings and interest can help retirees build wealth faster. If you talk to a financial expert or an investment professional, they can help you come up with a long-term investment plan that fits your retirement goals.

Investment plans are important if you want to have a comfortable retirement. Key parts of a successful investment strategy are diversifying your investment portfolio, looking into different investment options, knowing asset allocation and risk management, and focusing on long-term wealth accumulation. By carefully thinking about their risk tolerance, goals, and time frame, retirees can build a portfolio that fits their needs and helps them make enough money to live comfortably. Adopt the power of strategic investing and you'll be on your way to long-term financial security when you leave.

Entrepreneurship and Small Business Ventures

People in retirement have a special chance to try out entrepreneurship and start their own small businesses. This chapter goes into detail about starting a business after retirement. It talks about the possible possibilities, how important it is to find market gaps and make a business plan, and how to deal with the challenges and benefits of being a business owner at this time in your life.

Exploring Entrepreneurial Opportunities:
When you retire, you have the time and freedom to start your own business. It gives people a place to turn their hobbies, interests, and skills into money-making businesses. Retirees can find business chances by finding gaps in the market, figuring out what consumers want, and looking into new trends. Retirees can find narrow markets and start businesses that meet specific needs by using their experience, skills, and networks.

Creating a Business Plan:
If you want to be successful as an entrepreneur, you need a good business plan. Retirees who want to start a business should do a lot of study on their target market, figure out what makes them unique, and make a plan for their business. This includes figuring out how the business will be set up, doing a study of the competition, setting financial goals, and making plans for marketing and running the business. A well-written

business plan is like a road map that shows retirees how to start and grow their small business.

Challenges and Rewards:
Starting a business in retirement can be exciting, but it also comes with challenges. Retirees need to be ready to change to a changing business environment, handle financial risks, and take on the responsibilities that come with owning a business. This includes marketing their goods or services, handling finances, meeting legal and regulatory requirements, and building a customer base. But the benefits of being a business in retirement can be big. It gives you the chance to make money, follow your interests, and keep a sense of meaning and fulfillment.

Finding a Balance Between Owning a Business and the Lifestyle You Want in Retirement:
Finding a balance between owning a business and the lifestyle you want in retirement is an important part of being an entrepreneur in retirement. Retirees should look at their personal goals, time commitments, and financial goals to make sure their business idea fits with their general vision for retirement. Setting clear limits, giving tasks to other people, and making systems can help retirees run their businesses well while still enjoying their retirement.

Entrepreneurship and small business projects can be a great way to spend your retirement if you are looking for new challenges and opportunities. By thinking about ways to be an entrepreneur, making a thorough business plan, and figuring out how to handle the challenges of owning a business, retirees can build great businesses that fit with their interests, make money, and add to their overall happiness in retirement. With careful planning, persistence, and a willingness to accept change, being an entrepreneur in retirement can open up a new chapter of personal and financial growth.

Gig Economy and On-Demand Work

The gig economy and on-demand work sites have changed the way that people make money in the modern world. These flexible and easy-to-find chances give retirees a new way to make money and stay involved in the workforce. This chapter talks about the gig economy and on-demand work. It talks about the different kinds of jobs that are available in areas like ride-sharing, delivery services, freelance work, and online marketplaces. It also talks about how important it is to use your skills and have as much flexibility as possible to have a satisfying retirement.

Getting on board with the "gig economy":
The "gig economy" gives people a lot of ways to make money with their skills and resources. Ride-sharing services make it possible for retirees to use their cars to give rides on their own time. Delivery services give people the chance to send gifts and goods to different places and at different times. Freelance work lets retirees use their skills to help people in areas like writing, graphic design, coaching, and more. Online markets give retirees a place to sell their goods, crafts, or other unique

items to customers all over the world. Getting involved in the gig economy gives retirees a lot of ways to make money while still being in charge of their work.

Exploring On-Demand Work Platforms:
On-demand work platforms have made it easier to look for and get gigs. Platforms like Uber, Lyft, DoorDash, Upwork, and Etsy connect retirees with people who want their services or goods. These platforms provide the infrastructure, customer base, and payment systems that seniors need to join the gig economy, making it easier for them to do so. By looking into these platforms, seniors can find a wide range of ways to make money using their skills and experience.

Maximizing Flexibility and Making the Most of Your Skills:
One of the best things about the gig economy and on-demand work is that it gives you a lot of freedom. Retirees can choose when, where, and how much they want to work. This gives them the freedom to balance their work with their personal obligations and the way they want to spend their retirement. By putting their skills to use, retired people can offer specialized services that meet specific needs and charge more for them. This gives seniors the freedom and flexibility of the gig economy while still letting them use their skills and experience.

How to Have a Satisfying Retirement: Embracing the gig economy and on-demand work can help you have a satisfying retirement. Retirees can earn money while staying busy, involved, and connected to their communities. Because gig work is flexible, retirees can follow other interests, hobbies, or travel plans without putting their financial security at risk. It gives you a sense of meaning, success, and continued growth.

The gig economy and on-demand work platforms have changed the way people spend their retirement years by giving them easy and open ways to make money on their own terms. By embracing the gig economy, looking into on-demand work platforms, maximizing their flexibility, and making the most of their skills, retirees can create a fulfilling retirement experience that combines financial security with personal satisfaction. The gig economy gives retirees a lot of ways to keep busy, use their skills, and enjoy the perks of a flexible work-life balance. If you have the right attitude and are willing to change, the gig economy and on-demand work can be important parts of a rich and fulfilling retirement.

Balancing Income and Lifestyle

Retirement is not only about financial security but also about enjoying a fulfilling lifestyle. Achieving a balance between income generation and maintaining a satisfying retirement lifestyle is crucial. This chapter delves into the importance of striking the right balance, setting financial goals aligned with personal preferences, and considering the trade-offs between active and passive income sources. By finding the perfect equilibrium, retirees can ensure financial stability while enjoying the lifestyle they desire.

Setting Financial Goals:

To strike a balance between income and lifestyle in retirement, it is essential to establish clear financial goals. These goals should encompass both short-term and long-term objectives. Short-term goals might include covering living expenses, healthcare costs, and leisure activities. Long-term goals may involve legacy planning and ensuring a comfortable retirement for the years to come. By defining these goals, retirees can better evaluate income opportunities and make informed decisions about their financial strategies.

Evaluating Income Opportunities:

When assessing income opportunities in retirement, it is important to consider personal preferences and priorities. Retirees should evaluate potential sources of income based on factors such as time commitment, enjoyment, and alignment with their skills and interests. Some may prefer part-time work or freelance gigs that allow for flexibility and engagement, while others may prioritize passive income streams that provide a steady flow of funds without requiring constant active involvement. By aligning income opportunities with personal preferences, retirees can ensure that their financial endeavors enhance their overall retirement experience.

Considering Trade-offs:

Retirees must recognize the trade-offs associated with different income sources. Active income streams, such as part-time jobs or freelance work, may provide immediate cash flow and a sense of purpose, but they require time and effort. Passive income sources, on the other hand, may require upfront investment and time to build but can eventually provide a more hands-off approach to generating income. Retirees need to weigh these trade-offs based on their lifestyle preferences, risk tolerance, and desired level of involvement. A diversified approach that combines active and passive income sources can provide a well-rounded financial strategy that supports both income needs and a fulfilling retirement lifestyle.

Striking the Perfect Equilibrium:

Finding the perfect equilibrium between income and lifestyle in retirement is a personal journey. It requires a thoughtful evaluation of financial goals, income opportunities, and trade-offs. Retirees must assess their priorities, considering factors such as financial security, personal fulfillment, and work-life balance. It may involve making adjustments along the way as circumstances change or new opportunities arise. Striking the right balance allows retirees to enjoy the fruits of their labor while maintaining a lifestyle that brings them joy, purpose, and contentment.

Achieving a harmonious balance between income generation and lifestyle is a vital aspect of retirement planning. By setting clear financial goals, evaluating income opportunities based on personal preferences, and considering trade-offs between active and passive income sources, retirees can create a fulfilling retirement experience. Striking the perfect equilibrium ensures both financial stability and the ability to enjoy a rewarding lifestyle in retirement. With careful consideration and thoughtful planning, retirees can navigate the complexities of income and lifestyle to create a retirement journey that is both financially prosperous and personally fulfilling.

By exploring these innovative income generation strategies, you can create a diverse portfolio of income streams that provide financial stability and freedom in retirement. In the next chapter, we will explore smart investment principles that will help you grow your wealth and secure a prosperous future.

Get ready to unlock the secrets of successful investing in Chapter 5: Wealth Building and Investment Strategies.

6

Wealth Building and Investment Strategies

In Chapter 5, we delve into the realm of wealth building and investment strategies that can help you grow your financial assets and secure a prosperous future. By understanding and implementing smart investment principles, you can make your money work for you and accelerate your journey towards financial independence in retirement.

The Power of Compound Interest

Compound interest is a financial event that can have a big effect on how much money people have over time. This piece explains what compound interest is, how it works, and what you can do to get the most out of it. People can set themselves up for long-term financial success and comfort if they understand and use the power of compounding.

Understanding Compound Interest:

Compound interest is the idea that you can earn interest on both the capital amount and the interest that has already been earned. Compound interest is different from simple interest, which is only based on the capital. Over time, compound interest allows for exponential growth. This result can make it a lot easier to build up wealth, especially if investments are kept for a long time.

Long-Term Effect on Building Wealth:

Compound interest has a huge effect on building wealth over time. Even small gifts made regularly over time can add up to a lot of money. The earlier people start spending and letting their money grow on its own, the more likely they are to get rich. This is because the compounding effect makes it possible to make money from money, causing a snowball effect that speeds up the growth of wealth over time.

Exploring Compounding Strategies:

There are many ways to use the power of compound interest as an investment. One popular choice is to invest in the stock market, where the compounding effect is helped by dividends and capital growth. Bonds, mutual funds, and exchange-traded funds (ETFs) can also help you grow your money by adding to it. When using compounding strategies, it is important to do a lot of study, spread out investments, and think about how much risk you are willing to take.

How to Get the Most Out of Compound Interest:

To get the most out of compound interest, you need to start early and keep going. For capital to grow through compounding, time is a very important factor. By starting early, people give their investments more time to make money and take advantage of the effect of compounding. Consistency is also important because regular contributions or reinvesting profits make the growth potential bigger over time.

Compound interest is a strong way to build wealth over a long period of time. By knowing the idea of compound interest and how it leads to exponential growth, people can make better decisions about how to handle their money. People can get the most out of compound interest by looking into different ways to use it, starting early, and staying consistent. Using the power of compound interest can help you plan for a more safe and prosperous future, whether you want to save for retirement, pay for school, or reach other financial goals.

Building a Diversified Investment Portfolio

Building a diversified portfolio of investments is a key part of good financial planning. This piece goes into depth about how important it is to diversify, looks at different types of assets, and stresses how important it is to build a well-balanced portfolio. By diversifying their investments, people can improve their financial security, reduce risk, and make the most of their growth potential.

Diversification is the strategy of spreading investments across different asset classes, industries, and geographic areas. Its main goal is to lower risk by not putting too much money into one business. Diversification lets people lessen the effects of market volatility and lessen the bad things that could happen to any one purchase. It is a key part of making smart decisions about investments.

Understanding the Different Asset Classes:
To build a diverse portfolio of investments, people need to know about the different asset classes. Stocks give you control in a public company and give you the chance for your money to grow. Bonds, on the other hand, are forms of debt that pay interest on a regular basis. Investing in real estate gives you the chance to get rental income and see your property value go up. Also, unusual investments like commodities, hedge funds, and private equity give you more ways to spread your money around.

Putting together a well-balanced portfolio means taking into account a person's risk level, financial goals, and time frame. It brings together different types of assets to get the best variety. People can reduce the risk of market fluctuations by spreading their investments across asset types that haven't been linked together in the past. For example, when stocks don't do well, purchases in bonds or real estate may be more stable. In the same way, stocks or other investments may have more growth potential than bonds when bond returns are low.

Strategic Allocation and Rebalancing:
In strategic asset allocation, you figure out how much of each asset class you should have based on your goals and how much risk you are willing to take. It makes sure that investments

are spread out evenly. To keep the desired asset distribution, the portfolio needs to be watched and rebalanced on a regular basis. Rebalancing means selling assets that have done well and putting the money into ones that have done poorly. This helps keep the desired risk-return balance.

Risk Management and Potential for Growth:
Diversification is a tool for risk management because it reduces the amount of money that is put into a single investment or industry. It helps protect against big losses and makes it more likely that long-term returns will be good. A diverse portfolio also has a chance of growing because different types of assets do well at different times. By diversifying, people put themselves in a position to take advantage of growth opportunities in multiple industries and asset classes.

Diversifying your investments is a smart and effective way to make your finances more stable and get the most out of your growth potential. Diversification lets people control risk, lower volatility, and take advantage of opportunities across different types of assets. People can confidently navigate the investment world if they understand the value of diversification, try out different asset classes, and build a well-balanced portfolio that fits their risk tolerance and financial goals. Diversification is a key part of smart investment planning that helps ensure long-term financial protection and success.

Setting Clear Investment Goals

Setting clear business goals is one of the most important things you can do to get ahead financially. This chapter talks about how important it is to set clear business goals and time frames, set short-term and long-term financial goals, and make a plan for how to reach those goals. By setting clear investment goals, people can create a strategic framework that guides their investment choices and keeps them on the path to financial success.

Setting Clear Investment Goals:
　The first step to setting clear investment goals is to figure out what your investment goals are. Do you want your money to grow, do you want a steady income, or do you want both? Knowing what you want to get out of your investments will help you choose the right vehicles and tactics that will help you reach your financial goals. It's also important to think about how much time you have. Short-term goals, like saving for a down payment on a house, may require investments with less risk and more cash. Long-term goals, like saving for retirement, can handle a higher risk tolerance and investments that focus on growth.

Identifying Short-Term and Long-Term Financial Goals:
　It is important to know both short-term and long-term financial goals in order to set clear business goals. Short-term goals usually involve reaching certain financial milestones within a few years, like paying off debt, saving up for a trip,

or starting an emergency fund. Long-term goals, on the other hand, are larger financial goals that last longer than ten years, like paying for college, retiring comfortably, or leaving money to future generations. By making these goals clear, people can set up the foundation for their investing strategy.

Making a Roadmap to Reach Investment Goals:
Once investment goals have been set, it's important to make a road map. This means making a step-by-step plan that shows what needs to be done to reach each goal. Start by looking at your current cash situation and figuring out how far you are from where you want to be. Then, break the big goals down into smaller, more doable steps that can be reached over time. Give each milestone a clear schedule and a set of goals that can be measured. Also, think about the types of investments and strategies that will help you reach each goal, such as diversifying your portfolio, putting money into retirement accounts, or looking into real estate or stock investment possibilities. Review your plan often and make changes to it as needed to account for changes in your finances or the market.

Setting clear investment goals also involves keeping an eye on success and making any changes that are needed along the way. Review your financial portfolio often to make sure it still fits your goals and level of risk tolerance. Check your roadmap every so often to see how far you've come toward each milestone and make any course changes you need. Both the financial markets and your own life can change, so it's important to be adaptable and change your investment plan as needed. If you need to, talk to a professional about your spending plan to make sure it stays on track.

Understanding Risk and Reward

To make good investment choices, you need to know how risk and reward relate to each other. This chapter talks about the risk-return tradeoff, figuring out how much risk you can handle, and coming up with a good investment plan. It also shows how important asset allocation and variety are for controlling risk. By understanding these key ideas, people can confidently manage the investment world and increase their chances of getting good returns.

Evaluating the Risk-Return Tradeoff:
 The risk-return tradeoff is one of the most important ideas in investing. It says that in general, bigger returns come with higher levels of risk. Before making decisions about investments, it is important to weigh this choice. Investing in stocks or developing markets, which have the potential for higher returns, comes with a higher level of risk, such as price volatility and market changes. On the other hand, investments with less risk, like government bonds or money market funds, tend to have smaller returns. By understanding this relationship, investors can decide how much risk they are willing to take to get the results they want.

Assessing Your Risk Tolerance:
 One of the most important steps in creating a good invest-

ment plan is to figure out how much risk you are willing to take. Risk tolerance is how comfortable a person is with taking risks with their money. Risk tolerance is affected by a person's financial situation, business goals, time horizon, and personality. Conservative investors with a low risk tolerance may want to protect their capital and choose less volatile investments, while aggressive investors with a higher risk tolerance may be more willing to take on more market exposure for the chance of higher yields. If you know how much danger you are willing to take, you can choose investments that fit with your level of comfort and your financial goals.

Creating an Appropriate Investment Strategy:

It is important to create an appropriate investment strategy after figuring out how much risk you are willing to take. This plan should think about both the risks and the rewards. Conservative investors may focus on assets that generate income, like bonds or stocks that pay dividends, to get stable results with little risk. Moderately conservative investors may put some of their money into growth-oriented investments like blue-chip stocks or balanced mutual funds to find a mix between stability and growth. A big part of an aggressive investor's portfolio might be made up of high-risk, high-reward investments like small-cap stocks or unusual assets. By matching your investment plan to how much risk you're willing to take, you can find a good balance between possible returns and exposure to risk.

Managing Risk with Asset Allocation and Diversification:

Asset allocation and diversification are two good ways to handle risk. To create a balanced portfolio, asset allocation means spreading investments across different asset types, such as stocks, bonds, real estate, and commodities. Diversification, on the other hand, means spreading investments across each asset class so that the success of each investment doesn't affect the portfolio as a whole as much. By spreading out their investments, investors can lower the risk that comes with losing money in one security or sector and making money in another. This approach helps keep risks in check and could improve long-term returns.

Understanding the risk-return tradeoff, figuring out how much risk you are willing to take, and coming up with a good investment plan are all important for investing success. By looking at the relationship between risk and return, investors can make choices that are in line with their goals and how much risk they are willing to take. Creating a good investment plan makes sure that investments are suited to each person's needs and goals. Managing risk through asset allocation and diversification can help financial portfolios be less affected by changes in the market. By using these ideas when making investment decisions, people can confidently navigate the complicated investment landscape and increase their chances of getting good returns while managing risk well.

Investing in Stocks and Equities

Investing in stocks and equities gives people a chance to take part in the growth and success of business. This chapter talks about the basics of investing in the stock market. It also talks about different ways to invest, like value investing, growth investing, and dividend investing, and it stresses how important it is to do a lot of study and analysis before making investment decisions.

Understanding the Basics of Investing in the Stock Market:

When you invest in the stock market, you buy shares of publicly traded companies and become a part-owner of those companies. Stocks are shares of a company, and they can give you money back in the form of capital gains and income. It's important to know how to use key stock market terms like market capitalization, price-to-earnings ratio, and dividend yield because they tell you about the size, value, and dividend payment of a company. Also, getting to know stock market indices like the S&P 500 or the Dow Jones Industrial Average helps buyers keep track of how the market is doing as a whole.

Looking at different ways to invest:

Value investing is all about finding undervalued stocks that are selling for less than their true value. Investors who use this strategy look at a company's financial records, evaluate its position in the market, and look for opportunities where the stock price doesn't match the real value of the business. By buying undervalued stocks, value buyers hope to make money when the market realizes what the company is really worth.

Investing for growth means putting money into companies that have a good chance of growing in the future. Investors who use this approach look for companies whose sales and earnings are growing faster than average. Growth investors are most interested in companies that are in industries that are growing quickly or that have new goods or services. The goal is to make money off of the company's rising value as its earnings and market share grow over time.

Dividend investing means putting your money into companies that regularly give their shareholders a part of their profits as dividends. Investors in dividends look for stable companies that have always paid dividends and have the chance for dividends to grow. By buying dividend-paying stocks, buyers hope to get a steady stream of income and share in the long-term success of the company.

Conducting Thorough Research and Analysis:
  It is important to do thorough research and analysis before making investment choices. Investors should look at a company's sales growth, profitability, debt levels, and cash flow to figure out how healthy it is financially. It is also important to evaluate the company's competitors, business trends, and management team. Investors should read annual reports, financial statements, and analyst reports to learn more and make choices that are well-informed. Investors can also find risks and opportunities that could affect the success of stocks by keeping an eye on macroeconomic factors and market trends.

When people invest in stocks and shares, they get a chance to take part in the growth and success of companies. By learning the basics of investing in the stock market and trying out different investment strategies, investors can make their method fit their financial goals and how much risk they are willing to take. Before making an investment, investors should do a lot of study and analysis. This helps them make smart choices and get the best possible returns. By making a well-thought-out investment plan and keeping a close eye on the market, investors can confidently manage the stock market and increase their chances of long-term investment success.

Fixed Income Investments: Bonds and Treasury Securities

Exploring the world of fixed income investments and their role in a diversified portfolio.

Understanding the different types of bonds and treasury securities.

Evaluating the risk and return characteristics of fixed income investments.

Fixed-income investments are a key part of having a diversified portfolio of investments. This chapter focuses on bonds and treasury assets to look at the world of fixed income investments. It explains what these financial instruments are, what their different types are, and how risky and profitable they are.

Bonds and government securities:

Bonds: Bonds are forms of debt that states, cities, and businesses use to raise money. When an investor buys a bond, they are basically giving the issuer money in exchange for regular interest payments and the return of the principal amount at maturity. The coupon rates, maturity dates, and face prices of bonds are all set ahead of time. Bonds can be put into different groups, such as government bonds, municipal bonds, business bonds, and convertible bonds. Each type has its own risk and return profile.

Treasury assets are bonds that the U.S. Department of the Treasury sells to pay for government spending. These assets are considered low-risk investments because the U.S. government backs them with its full faith and credit. Treasury bills (T-bills), treasury notes (T-notes), and treasury bonds (T-bonds) are the three main types of treasury assets. T-bills mature in less than a year, while T-notes and T-bonds mature over a longer period of time, from two to thirty years. Most people think of Treasury assets as safe investments, and they are often used as a standard for other fixed-income investments.

Taking a look at the risk and return:

Fixed-income assets vary in terms of risk and return based on the issuer, the quality of the credit, and the length of the investment. Bond investors pay close attention to the risk of default, which means that the issuer might not be able to make interest payments on time or pay back the capital. Most of the time, bonds with better credit ratings are thought to be less risky, while bonds with lower credit ratings have higher yields but a higher chance of default. As they are backed by the U.S.

government, Treasury assets are thought to have the lowest risk of not being paid back.

Most of the return on investments with a set income comes from interest payments, which are also called "coupon payments." The dividend rate is usually set when the bond is issued and stays the same for its whole life. The return on fixed-income investments relies on the state of the market, the interest rates at the time, and the issuer's creditworthiness. When interest rates change, the market value of assets that pay a fixed income may also change. Interest rates and bond prices go in opposite directions. When interest rates go up, bond prices tend to go down, and vice versa.

Fixed-income investments, like bonds and treasury securities, give buyers the chance to earn a steady income and keep their money safe. When investors know the different kinds of bonds and treasury securities, they can adjust their fixed income allocation to fit their risk tolerance and financial goals. In order to build a well-balanced portfolio, it is important to look at the risk and return of fixed income assets. Investors can find the right mix between risk and return in the fixed income asset class by carefully considering credit quality, duration, and current market conditions.

Real Estate Investment Strategies

People often buy in real estate as a way to get rich and diversify their portfolios. This chapter looks at ways to invest in real estate that go beyond buying rental homes. It looks at other choices, like real estate investment trusts (REITs) and real estate crowdfunding, and evaluates the risks and rewards that might come with them.

REITs, or real estate investment trusts, are worth looking into.

REITs are a type of business vehicle that pools money from many investors to buy a portfolio of real estate properties that generate income. They are traded publicly on stock exchanges and give individual investors the chance to own real estate without having to own the land directly.

Types of REITs: REITs can be put into different groups based on the types of real estate assets they own. These include both equity REITs and mortgage REITs. Equity REITs own and run buildings that bring in money, and mortgage REITs help pay for real estate projects. There are also REITs that focus on specific types of properties, like residential, business, industrial, or healthcare properties.

Benefits of REITs: There are many good things about investing in REITs. First, they give investors access to many different types of real estate and real estate areas. Second, REITs make regular money through rent payments and property cash flows. This money is usually given to investors as rewards. Lastly, because their shares can be bought and sold on stock markets, REITs provide liquidity.

The Crowdfunding of Real Estate:
Crowdfunding for real estate involves putting together money from many people to pay for real estate projects. These investments are made easier by online platforms, which let individual investors take part in real estate projects that were once only open to institutional investors.

There are two main kinds of real estate crowdfunding: those that are based on equity and those that are based on debt. Equity-based crowdfunding is when people put money into a real estate project and get a cut of the income. Debt-based crowdfunding means lending money to real estate developers or property owners and getting set interest payments over a certain amount of time.

Benefits of Real Estate Crowdfunding:
Investors can get a lot out of real estate crowdfunding. It gives investors access to a bigger range of real estate projects, which lets them spread out their investments. It also gives investors the chance to put their money into projects that match their tastes and willingness to take risks. Also, most real estate crowdfunding platforms are open, so investors can see how their money is doing and make choices based on that information.

Assessing Risks and Rewards:
All real estate investments, such as REITs and real estate crowdfunding, have risks and possible rewards that come with

them. Among the most important things to think about are:

Market risk:
The value of real estate can change depending on the market, the economy, and the way supply and demand work. Changes in interest rates can also have an effect on how well an investment in real estate does.

Liquidity Risk:
REITs have liquidity because they can be traded on the stock market, but real estate crowdfunding purchases may have less liquidity. Investors should carefully think about how they can get to their money in case something unexpected happens.

Management Risk:
Real estate investments require effective management to maintain and improve property values. Investors in REITs depend on teams of professionals to run the business. Investors in real estate crowdfunding, on the other hand, need to do research on the capabilities of the project sponsor.

Possible Rewards:
Rental income, property appreciation, and dividends are all ways that real estate purchases could pay off. These returns can give you income and give you the chance that your money will go up in value over time.

There are more ways to invest in real estate than just buying rental homes. REITs and real estate crowdfunding offer different ways for people to own real estate and possibly make money and see their investments grow in value. Understanding the benefits, risks, and rewards of these strategies is important for investors who want to make smart choices and diversify their real estate investment portfolios.

Alternative Investments and Asset Classes

Alternative investments have become more popular among investors who want to diversify their portfolios and potentially get better returns. This chapter talks about commodities, rare metals, cryptocurrencies, and venture capital as alternatives to traditional investments. It also stresses how important it is to understand the unique features and risks of these investments and decide if they are right for you based on your financial goals and how much risk you are willing to take.

Investigating Other Investment Options:

Commodities: Commodities are things that can be seen and touched, like oil, natural gas, corn, wheat, gold, silver, and other metals. Investing in commodities can be done through commodity futures contracts, exchange-traded funds (ETFs), or owning the physical goods themselves.

Precious Metals:

Gold, silver, platinum, and palladium are all examples of precious metals. They are thought to be good ways to save money and protect against inflation. Investors can buy these metals in the form of coins, ETFs, or stocks in mining companies.

Cryptocurrencies:

Bitcoin, Ethereum, and Litecoin are examples of cryptocurrencies, which are a new type of product. These digital currencies are based on blockchain technology and have the potential for high profits. However, they are also very volatile and have risks related to government regulation. Investors can directly buy and hold cryptocurrencies or invest in funds that focus on cryptocurrencies.

Venture capital:

With venture capital, you invest in young companies that have a lot of room to grow. This type of investment gives you the chance to take part in innovative new businesses, but it also comes with a lot of risks because early-stage businesses fail so often. Most investors get into venture capital through special funds or angel investment.

Getting to know the unique qualities and risks

Volatility and Lack of Liquidity:

Compared to traditional assets like stocks and bonds, alternative investments are often more volatile and have less liquidity. The prices of commodities, rare metals, and cryptocurrencies can change a lot, and it may be hard to sell investments or get out of them.

Regulatory and legal risks:

Some alternative investments, like cryptocurrencies and venture capital, work in less regulated settings. This means that they are more likely to be affected by changes in regulations and may be more vulnerable to fraud or security risks.

Limited Transparency:
Investors may not have much information about alternative investments, which can make it hard to correctly judge their value and performance.

Suitability and Portfolio Allocation

Financial Goals and Risk Tolerance:
When deciding between different options, investors should think about their financial goals, how much time they have, and how much risk they are willing to take. These investments can help diversify your portfolio and give you the chance to make more money, but they also come with more risk.

Portfolio Allocation:
Alternative investments should be part of a well-balanced portfolio that also includes traditional assets. Alternative investments should be used in a way that fits with a person's risk profile and financial goals. To figure out the best way to divide up your assets, you should talk to a financial adviser.

Alternative investments give investors a chance to diversify their holdings in ways that aren't possible with traditional asset classes. Commodities, precious metals, cryptocurrencies, and venture capital all have the ability to give investors higher returns, but they also have more risks and are harder to understand. Understanding the features and risks of different investments is important if you want to make smart investment decisions that match your financial goals and level of risk tolerance.

Monitoring and Adjusting Your Portfolio

Once you have a well-diversified mix of investments, it is important to keep an eye on how it is doing and make changes as needed. This chapter talks about how important it is to keep a disciplined approach to monitoring your portfolio, evaluating the success of your investments, and making the right changes to keep your desired asset allocation.

Taking a disciplined approach to monitoring the portfolio

Set Clear Metrics and Benchmarks for Monitoring:
    Set clear metrics and benchmarks to track how your business is doing. This could involve keeping track of the results of the whole portfolio, comparing them to relevant market indices, and judging how well each investment is doing.

Regular Review Schedule:

Set up a regular time to look over your resume. This could be done once a month, three times a year, or once a year, based on what you want and how complicated your investments are. Reviewing your investments on a regular basis keeps you up to date on market trends and how well your stocks are doing.

Keep up with financial news, economic factors, and industry trends that could affect your investments. This information will help you make smart choices and figure out what opportunities or risks might be out there.

How to Measure the Success of an Investment

Measure Against Goals:
Compare the success of your investments to the goals and objectives you set for your money. Check to see if your stock is on the right track to help you reach your long-term goals.

Risk-Adjusted Returns:
When judging the success of an investment, you should look at the risk-adjusted returns. It's important to figure out how much chance you took to get the money back from your investments.

Compare the performance of your investments to useful benchmarks, like market indices or groups of similar investments. This study helps you figure out if your investments are doing better or worse than similar assets.

Making the Needed Changes

Rebalancing:
Check your asset allocation on a regular basis to make sure it fits with your risk profile and financial goals. When you rebalance, you buy or sell assets to get your portfolio back to its goal allocation. This helps keep things varied and keeps risks under control.

Choosing investments:
Look at the success of each investment in your portfolio. If an investment keeps losing money or no longer fits with your investment theory, you might want to replace it with a better one.

Market Conditions:
When making changes to your stock, you should think about macroeconomic factors, market trends, and how investors' feelings are changing. Changes may be needed to keep up with changes in the market or to take advantage of new possibilities.

Monitoring and making changes to your investment account is an ongoing process that makes sure it stays in line with your financial goals and how much risk you are willing to take. You can keep a well-balanced and optimized portfolio by taking a structured approach to monitoring your portfolio, evaluating the success of your investments, and making any necessary changes. By looking at your finances often and making changes, you can set yourself up for long-term success and deal well with changing market conditions.

By applying these wealth building and investment strategies, you can create a robust investment portfolio that aligns with your financial goals and risk tolerance. In the next chapter, we will address the importance of maintaining good health and well-being in retirement.

Get ready to explore strategies for a healthy and fulfilling retirement in Chapter 6: Prioritizing Health and Wellness.

7

Prioritizing Health and Wellness

In Chapter 6, we shift our focus to the importance of prioritizing health and wellness in retirement. A fulfilling retirement goes beyond financial security; it encompasses physical and mental well-being. Let's explore strategies and practices that will help you maintain optimal health and lead a fulfilling life in your golden years.

The Importance of Physical Activity

Physical exercise is one of the most important parts of a healthy lifestyle, and it plays a key role in promoting general health and longevity. This chapter talks about the many benefits of exercise, looks at different types of physical activities that are good for different levels of fitness, and stresses how important it is to make an exercise plan that fits your skills and interests.

Benefits of working out regularly

Physical Health:
Regular exercise helps you keep a healthy weight, strengthens your muscles and bones, improves your heart health, and makes you physically fitter overall. It lowers the chance of getting long-term diseases like heart disease, diabetes, and some kinds of cancer.

Mental Health:
Working out has a big effect on your mental health. It makes your body make endorphins, which are "feel-good" hormones that make you feel better and less anxious or depressed. Regular physical exercise is also linked to better brain function and a better ability to deal with stress.

Longevity:
Studies show over and over that people who exercise regularly live longer and have a better quality of life. Exercise keeps older people from getting weaker with age, improves their ability to do things, and gives them more energy and freedom.

Looking at Different Kinds of Physical Activities

Aerobic Exercise:
Walking quickly, jogging, cycling, swimming, and dancing

are all examples of aerobic workouts that raise the heart rate and strengthen the heart and blood vessels. These activities are good for people with different levels of fitness and can be changed to fit each person's tastes and abilities.

Strength Training:
Adding resistance training exercises, like weightlifting or bodyweight exercises, helps build muscle strength and stamina. Strength training is important for keeping your muscle mass, making your bones denser, and improving your general fitness.

Exercises for Flexibility and Balance:
Stretching, yoga, and tai chi all help increase flexibility, improve joint motion, and improve balance and coordination. These tasks are especially good for older people because they make them less likely to fall and keep them mobile.

Creating a personalized workout plan

Assessing your fitness level: Before you start an exercise program, you should look at your present fitness level and talk to a doctor or nurse, especially if you have any health problems.

Setting Goals:
Set clear goals based on the results you want, whether it's to lose weight, improve your endurance, get stronger, or improve your general health. Setting goals that can be reached helps you stay motivated and keep track of your progress.

Variety and fun:

Include a variety of physical tasks in your routine to keep it interesting and keep you from getting bored. Choose team sports, outdoor activities, group fitness classes, or solo workouts that you enjoy and that fit your hobbies.

Gradual Progression:

Start with a strength and length of time that you can handle, and then gradually increase both over time. This lets your body change and lessens the chance of getting hurt.

Consistency:

To get the most out of exercise, you need to be consistent. Aim for regular exercise, preferably at least 150 minutes of moderate-intensity physical activity or 75 minutes of vigorous-intensity activity per week, plus strength training exercises twice a week.

Regular physical exercise is important for keeping your overall health, improving your mental health, and living longer. By trying out different types of physical activities that are good for different levels of fitness and making a personalized exercise plan, people can get the benefits of exercise while making it fun and easy to keep up. Getting regular exercise is an investment in your health and happiness in the long run.

Healthy Eating and Nutrition

Exploring the impact of nutrition on overall health and well-being.
Understanding the principles of a balanced and nutritious diet.
Incorporating healthy eating habits and making informed food choices.

Nutrition is a key part of supporting health and well-being all around. This chapter looks at how nutrition affects our physical and mental health. It explains the basics of a healthy, balanced diet and stresses how important it is to develop healthy eating habits and make smart food choices.

How nutrition affects health and happiness

Health of the body:
A healthy, well-balanced meal gives you the nutrients, vitamins, and minerals you need to keep your body running well. It helps you keep a healthy weight, helps your body grow and develop properly, boosts your immune system, and lowers your risk of chronic diseases like obesity, diabetes, heart disease, and some cancers.

Mental Health:
The food we eat also has a big effect on how healthy our minds are. Research shows that people who eat a healthy diet full of fruits, veggies, whole grains, and lean proteins are less likely to get depressed or anxious. On the other hand, eating

a lot of prepared foods, sugary snacks, and fats that aren't good for you may make you more likely to have mental health problems.

Basics of a well-balanced and healthy diet

Variety: By eating things from many different food groups, you make sure your body gets a wide range of nutrients. Fruits, veggies, whole grains, lean proteins, healthy fats, and low-fat dairy or alternatives to dairy should all be part of your diet.

Measure: Watch your portions and eat everything in measure. Pay attention to the size of your portions to keep a good energy balance and avoid overeating.

Whole Foods: Instead of highly processed and packed foods, choose whole foods that haven't been changed much. Whole foods usually have more nutrients and less extra sugars, preservatives, and additives.

Nutrient Density: Give priority to foods that are "nutrient dense," which means they have a lot of nutrients for how many calories they have. Include foods like fruits, vegetables, legumes, nuts, and seeds in your diet to make sure you get a wide range of important nutrients.

Getting into the habit of eating well

Meal planning: Plan your meals ahead of time to make sure you have a balanced and healthy diet all week. Include a range of foods from different food groups, and if you want to save time and make healthier choices, you might want to think about meal prepping.

Mindful Eating: To practice mindful eating, pay attention

to your body's signals for when you are hungry and when you are full. Eat slowly, enjoying each bite, and pay attention to how the food tastes, feels, and makes you feel.

Hydration: Drink enough water throughout the day to keep yourself from getting dehydrated. Try to drink less sugary drinks and more water, herbal tea, or flavored water instead.

How to Choose Food Wisely

Reading Labels: Read the labels on prepared foods to find out how healthy they are. Pay attention to the size of the portion, the amount of added sugar, the amount of sodium, and any artificial additives or preservatives.

Food Quality: Whenever you can, choose fresh, high-quality foods that come from your own area. Focus on organic veggies and choose meats and seafood that are lean, organic, and from sources that are good for the environment.

Get an education: Read reliable sources, talk to registered dietitians, and stay up to date on nutritional rules to learn more about nutrition. Be skeptical of diet trends and false information about nutrition.

Adopting good eating habits and making smart food choices are important for a person's health and well-being as a whole. People can get the most out of their nutrition and enjoy the benefits of a healthy living if they understand how nutrition affects their physical and mental health and follow the rules of a balanced and healthy diet. Remember that even small changes in the way you eat can have a big effect on your health in the long run, and it's never too late to start eating better.

Mental and Cognitive Stimulation

Retirement is a new part of life that can be used to grow as a person, including by keeping your mind and brain active. This chapter talks about how important it is to do things in retirement that test and stimulate the brain. It talks about the benefits of mental and cognitive stimulation, gives examples of tasks that are good for brain health, and stresses how mindfulness and meditation can help improve mental health.

Why Mental and Cognitive Stimulation is Important

Brain Health: Doing things that make you think helps keep your brain healthy and busy. Research shows that mental stimulation may slow the onset of age-related cognitive disorders like Alzheimer's disease and dementia.

Cognitive Skills: Regular mental stimulation can help improve cognitive skills like remembering, focus, problem-solving, and making decisions. It improves the links between nerve cells and helps new brain cells grow. This makes the mind more resilient and flexible.

Activities to keep your mind and brain active

Puzzles and Games: Solve crossword puzzles, Sudoku, and jigsaw puzzles, or play strategy board games that require you to think critically and solve problems. These things test the brain and help keep it in good shape.

Reading and Learning: Read about things that interest you in books, newspapers, or magazines. Take classes, go to workshops, or do online training to keep learning throughout your life. Learning new skills or gaining new knowledge keeps the brain active and helps people grow as people.

Hobbies and creative activities: Try drawing, writing, playing a musical instrument, or gardening. These hobbies give people a way to express themselves, improve their cognitive skills, and make them feel more fulfilled.

Participate in group events, join clubs or organizations, or volunteer to keep in touch with other people. Social contacts are good for your brain, your emotions, and your ability to have intellectual conversations and learn from others.

Being aware and meditating

Mindfulness Practices: Do tasks that help you be more aware of the present moment and observe your thoughts and feelings without judging them. Practice being aware when you walk, eat, or do other things you do every day. This makes the mind clearer, lowers stress, and improves brain function.

Meditation: Add meditation to your daily routine to improve your ability to concentrate, focus, and feel good about yourself. Set aside time specifically for meditation. Start with short sessions and build up to longer ones. Meditation techniques like "focused attention" and "loving-kindness" can help people think better and feel better in general.

When you retire, you need to make mental and cognitive stimulation a top priority to keep your brain healthy, your cognitive skills sharp, and your general health good. Puzzles, reading, learning new skills, and interacting with other people are all brain-challenging tasks that can help build cognitive resilience and personal growth. Mindfulness and meditation also make you more clear-headed, lower stress, and improve your ability to think. By keeping their minds and brains active in retirement, people can continue to live full and intellectually rich lives.

Social Connections and Relationships

Retirement is a time of change that can be used to make new friends and deepen relationships with those you already have. This chapter talks about the importance of social connections in retirement. It talks about the benefits of keeping strong relationships and gives ideas for social events that can help people feel like they belong and are healthy.

Why it's important to have friends

Emotional health: Friendships, emotional support, and a sense of belonging are all things that come from having social ties. Strong relationships make people happier, reduce stress, and improve their general health and well-being. When you retire, your daily contacts may change, which makes it even more important to keep in touch with people.

Cognitive Health: Taking part in social activities and keeping in touch with people has been linked to better mental health and a lower chance of mental decline. Social interactions keep the brain active, lead to interesting conversations, and give people chances to learn and grow.

Getting involved in social things

Join Clubs and Groups: Look into area clubs, hobby groups, and groups that match your interests. By joining these groups, you can meet people with similar interests, do things together, and make new friends.

Free: Do free work or projects that help the community. Giving to a cause you care about not only helps other people, but it also gives you a chance to meet other workers and build relationships with them.

Attend Community Events: If you want to stay involved in your community, go to events like festivals, workshops, or speeches. These events give you the chance to meet new people, start talks, and make more friends.

Keeping relationships that matter alive

Family and Friends: Spend valuable time with your family and friends as a top priority. Set up regular get-togethers, trips, or shared activities that will help you connect and keep your relationships strong. Encourage open conversation and let your loved ones know how much you appreciate their help and love.

Peer Groups: Look for peer groups or social circles that are made for older people. These groups give people the chance to talk about the good and bad parts of retiring, share their own experiences, and go on trips together.

Technology and Social Media: Use technology and social media to stay in touch with friends and family, especially if you live far away or move around a lot. Use video calls, chat apps, and social media to close the distance and keep in touch regularly.

Having good relationships and social connections are important parts of a happy retirement. Participating in social activities, joining clubs or groups, and going to community events all help people feel like they belong and improve their emotional and mental health. Having close relationships with family, friends, and coworkers gives you support, company, and chances to grow as a person. By putting social ties first in retirement, people can build a strong social network that improves their quality of life as a whole.

Stress Management and Relaxation Techniques

Managing stress and putting relaxation first become very important for keeping emotional health when you retire. This chapter talks about how important it is to know how to deal with stress well. It also talks about different ways to relax and how important self-care tasks are for reducing stress and improving overall mental and emotional health.

Understanding Stress Management

Stress's effects: Long-term stress can be bad for both your physical and mental health, leading to things like anxiety, sadness, and heart problems. To keep your mental health in retirement, you need to know how important it is to deal with stress.

Effective Techniques for Managing Stress: Using stress management techniques helps people deal with pressures in a healthy way and live a more balanced, peaceful life. The goal of these methods is to reduce stress and build emotional strength.

Relaxation Techniques

Mindfulness and Meditation: When you practice mindfulness and meditation, you become more aware of the present moment. This helps you feel less stressed and more relaxed. With these methods, you focus on your breath, watch your thoughts without judging them, and let your mind rest in a calm state.

Deep breathing exercises, like diaphragmatic breathing, help turn on the relaxation reaction in the body. By slowing down their breathing and taking deep, controlled breaths, people can relieve stress, calm their nervous systems, and feel more at ease.

Yoga and Stretching: Gentle yoga poses and stretching routines can help release physical tension, make you more aware of your body, and help you relax. With these techniques, you move, control your breath, and pay attention to the present moment all at once.

Setting priorities for self-care

Get a hobby: Spend time doing things that bring you joy and satisfaction. Hobbies like drawing, gardening, reading, or playing an instrument can be relaxing, help you be more creative, and give you a way to express yourself.

Self-compassion means being kind to yourself and showing

yourself kindness. Treat yourself with love, forgiveness, and understanding. Self-care tasks like taking a bath, practicing self-reflection, or writing in a journal can improve emotional health and lower stress.

Maintain Healthy Lifestyle Habits: Make a healthy lifestyle a top priority by getting enough sleep, having a balanced diet, and exercising regularly. These habits are good for your general health, reduce stress, and make you stronger emotionally.

For mental health in retirement, it's important to know how to deal with stress and incorporate relaxation methods into daily life. Mindfulness, meditation, deep breathing routines, yoga, and doing things you enjoy are all good ways to relieve stress and calm down. Emotional resilience is also helped by making self-care tasks a priority and keeping healthy lifestyle habits. By doing these things, people can feel more peaceful, calm, and emotionally healthy in their retired years.

Sleep and Restorative Rest

Quality sleep and restorative rest are important for keeping your physical and mental health at its best, especially after you quit. This chapter talks about how important sleep is and gives tips on how to get healthy sleep habits. It also talks about how important it is to make a good sleeping setting and suggests getting professional help for sleep disturbances or disorders.

How Important Good Sleep Is

Physical Health: Getting enough sleep is important for the health and well-being of your body. It helps the immune system work better, helps keep hormones in balance, improves heart health, and helps people stay at a healthy weight. A good night's sleep helps the body feel refreshed, which lets it heal and fix itself.

Sleep is a very important part of both mental health and brain function. Getting enough sleep makes it easier to focus, remember, and make decisions. It also makes moods more stable and improves mental health, which makes anxiety and depression less likely.

Setting up good sleep habits

Consistent Sleep Schedule: Sleeping at the same time every night helps keep the body's internal clock in sync. Getting up and going to bed at the same time every day, even on the weekends, helps you sleep better and sets up a good sleep-wake cycle.

Setting up a relaxing bedtime routine: Doing something relaxing before bed can tell your body and mind that it's time to relax and get ready for sleep. Some ways to relax and get a better night's sleep are to read, take a warm bath, practice relaxation methods, or listen to soothing music.

Making a Sleep-Friendly setting: Creating a setting that is good for sleep can improve the quality of sleep. Make sure the bedroom is comfy, cool, dark, and quiet. Use comfortable bedding and spend money on a mattress and blankets that will support you. lessen the amount of time you spend on electronic devices before bed to lessen stimulation and help you sleep better.

Getting Help from a Professional

Find out if you have a sleep disorder: If you have trouble going asleep, staying asleep, or waking up feeling tired, this could be a sign that you have a sleep disorder. It is important to recognize and acknowledge these problems in order to get the right professional help.

Consulting a Health Care Provider: It is important to talk to a health care provider if sleep problems keep happening or have a big effect on how you live your daily life. They can look at the situation, give advice, and suggest actions or treatments that are right for each person.

In retirement, it's important to get good sleep and rest to keep your body and mind healthy. Setting up good sleep habits, such as a regular bedtime routine and sleep schedule, can improve the quality of sleep. Creating a good place to sleep can help you get a good night's rest. It's important to know the signs of sleep problems and get help from a professional when you need to. By making sleep and rest a priority, people can improve their general health, have better physical health, and have better mental and emotional health in their retirement years.

Preventive Health Care and Regular Check-ups

Preventive health care measures, like regular checkups, screenings, and vaccines, are important for staying healthy, especially for people who are retired. This chapter talks about how important preventive health care is, how important it is to talk to a doctor about a personalized health care plan, and how people should take care of chronic conditions and health issues as soon as they come up.

Why preventive health care is important

Early Detection and Intervention: Regular checkups and screenings make it possible to find potential health problems early, so that they can be treated and dealt with right away. When health problems are caught early, the result is often better and the prognosis is better.

Disease Prevention: Taking precautions like getting vaccinated and getting checked out can help keep some diseases from happening. Vaccinations guard against infectious diseases, and screenings like mammograms and colonoscopies can find early signs of cancer or other conditions.

Healthcare Professionals to Consult

Personalized health care plan: Everyone has different health needs, risks, and other things to think about. Talking to medical professionals, like primary care doctors or experts, can help you make a personalized health care plan that fits your needs. This plan could include suggestions for tests, vaccinations, changes to your lifestyle, and ways to deal with a disease.

Health Risk Assessment: People who work in health care can do thorough health risk assessments to find possible areas of worry and give the right advice. This assessment could include looking at the medical background of the family, how they live, and how their health is right now.

Taking charge of long-term conditions

Regular tracking: People with long-term conditions need to get regular checkups and tracking. This makes it easier to track how the situation is getting worse, change treatment plans as needed, and keep problems from happening. By keeping an eye on people on a regular basis, health care workers can offer ongoing support and guidance.

Lifestyle changes: Taking care of chronic conditions in a proactive way often means making changes to your lifestyle, like eating healthier, getting regular exercise, dealing with stress, and taking your medications as recommended. Health care workers can help people make changes to their lives that will last.

Problems with health are dealt with quickly

Timely Intervention: For the best health results, it is important to deal with health problems right away, whether they are new or old. Health problems can get worse or cause more problems if they are ignored or treated too slowly. It is very important to get medical help when you need it and to do what the doctor tells you to do.

Self-Advocacy: People should be bold and speak up for their own needs when it comes to their health care. This means asking questions, getting a second opinion when you need to, and knowing as much as you can about your own health and treatment choices.

Preventive health care and regular checkups are important parts of keeping your general health in good shape, especially during retirement. People can take charge of their health and make it more likely that they will have a healthy and fulfilling retirement by putting preventive health care first, getting personalized health care plans from medical professionals, managing chronic conditions proactively, and addressing health concerns quickly. A proactive approach to health care makes sure that problems are found early, treated quickly, and lead to better general health. This improves the quality of life in retirement.

Active Lifestyle and Hobbies

Keeping a busy lifestyle and doing things you enjoy are important parts of a happy retirement. This chapter talks about how important it is to stay busy, the benefits of having hobbies, and how important it is to find a good balance between relaxing and doing things in retirement.

Advantages of living an active life

Physical Health: Regular physical exercise is good for the heart, strengthens muscles and bones, improves flexibility and balance, and lowers the risk of chronic diseases like heart disease, diabetes, and osteoporosis. Keeping busy in retirement is good for your general health and improves your physical abilities.

Mental and emotional health: When you do physical activities, your body's natural "feel-good" hormones, called endorphins, are released. These hormones can make you feel happier and less anxious or depressed. A physically active lifestyle also improves brain function, memory, and mental clarity, which lowers the chance of age-related mental decline.

Why it's good to have hobbies

Joy and satisfaction: Hobbies are a way to express yourself, be creative, and grow as a person. Having a sense of purpose and general happiness in retirement is helped by doing things that bring you joy and satisfaction.

Social Connections: Hobbies often involve spending time with people who like the same things you do. This gives you the chance to meet new people and build important relationships. Participating in group activities or joining clubs or groups linked to a hobby can help you make new friends and feel like you belong to a group.

Getting a Good Balance

Variety of Activities: Trying out different activities and hobbies gives you a lot of different things to do and keeps retirement interesting and fun. This could mean doing artistic things like painting, writing, or playing an instrument, as well as sports, dancing, gardening, or giving back to the community.

Time to relax: It's important to stay busy, but it's also important to find time to relax and rest. Balance your physical activity with times of rest to improve your general health, avoid burnout, and feel refreshed.

Personalization and Flexibility: Every person has their own tastes and skills. It's important to pick activities and hobbies that match your interests, skills, and limits. Changing tasks to fit new situations keeps people interested and keeps them doing them.

An active living and doing things you enjoy are important parts of a happy retirement. Staying active is good for your body, mind, and emotions. It also improves your general health and quality of life in retirement. Hobbies bring happiness, satisfaction, and chances to meet new people. Finding a good mix between doing things and taking it easy is important for a healthy and enjoyable retirement. People can make the most of their retirement years and feel more purpose, joy, and satisfaction if they live an active lifestyle, try new things, and make time for both physical exercise and relaxation.

Emotional Well-being and Self-Care

Putting your mental health first and taking care of yourself are important parts of a happy retirement. This chapter talks about the importance of emotional health, the benefits of self-care tasks, and how important it is to get help when you need it.

How important emotional health is

Mental Health: Your emotional health has a direct effect on your mental health, including your ability to deal with stress, worry, and depression. Taking care of one's emotional well-being improves mental health and makes people more resilient, which makes retirement a better time.

Relationships: Being emotionally healthy makes it easier to get along with family, friends, and coworkers. When people are emotionally stable and happy, they can make relationships that are healthier and more meaningful. This helps them build a social network that will help them when they retire.

Benefits of doing things for yourself

Self-Reflection: Journaling, meditation, and mindfulness are all self-reflective activities that help people become more self-aware and think about themselves. These tasks give people a chance to think about their thoughts, feelings, and personal values, which helps them learn more about themselves.

Self-Expression: Doing creative things like art, music, or writing lets you express yourself and helps you talk to other people and let go of your feelings. When you retire, doing things that use your own interests and skills can improve your mental health and make you feel like you've accomplished something.

Self-Compassion: To practice self-compassion, you have to be kind to yourself, recognize your limits, and take care of yourself without judging yourself. Self-compassion-building activities, like taking breaks, setting limits, and putting self-care first, are good for emotional health and avoid burnout.

Seeking Support

Therapists and counselors: Getting help from a professional therapist or counselor can give you advice and ways to deal with mental problems. Therapy or counseling can help people deal with underlying problems, learn ways to deal with them, and keep their mental health in retirement.

Support Groups: When someone joins a support group or a peer-to-peer support network, they can meet other people who may have had similar experiences or problems. These groups give people a safe place to talk and get help, which helps them feel like they belong and lessens feelings of being alone.

Putting your mental health first and taking care of yourself are important parts of a happy retirement. People can improve their mental health and have a better quality of life in retirement by doing things that encourage self-reflection, self-expression, and self-compassion. When people go to therapists, counselors, or support groups when they need help, they get the tools and resources they need to deal with emotional problems and keep their mental health. By putting mental health first and taking care of themselves, people can really enjoy their retirement years to the fullest and feel more content, fulfilled, and happy overall.

By prioritizing your health and wellness, you can enjoy a vibrant and fulfilling retirement. In the next chapter, we will address the importance of creating a legacy and leaving a lasting impact.

Get ready to explore strategies for creating a meaningful and purposeful retirement in Chapter 7: Creating Your Legacy.

8

Creating Your Legacy

In Chapter 7, we delve into the concept of creating a legacy and leaving a lasting impact in retirement. Your retirement years present an opportunity to make a difference and contribute to the world in meaningful ways. Let's explore strategies for shaping your legacy and leaving behind a positive imprint on future generations.

Defining Your Personal Legacy

Defining your personal legacy is an introspective process that includes thinking about your values, beliefs, and principles that shape your identity and the impact you want to have on others. This chapter talks about the importance of leaving a lasting positive effect on loved ones, the community, and society as a whole. It also encourages people to think about themselves.

Thinking about Values, Principles, and Beliefs

Self-Reflection: Take some time to think about your personal values, beliefs, and principles that guide your actions and choices. Think about the things that make you who you are and the values you hold dear.

Life Experiences: Think about the big events in your life that have changed your outlook, morals, and personality. Find the lessons you've learned and the principles that have grown from them.

Finding the most important parts

What Matters Most: Figure out which parts of your life are the most important and meaningful to you. It could be family, relationships, education, giving back to the community, or anything else that fits your beliefs.

Passions and Skills: Think about your interests, skills, and gifts that help you grow as a person and help other people. How can you use these things to make a good difference?

Getting Clear on the Effect You Want

Loved Ones: Think about how you want to affect the people you care about. Think about how you can care for and help them, leave a legacy of love, and teach them values that will help them through life.

Think about how you want to affect the people in your neighborhood. How can you make your town better through volunteering, giving money, or being a leader? What change for the better do you want to make?

Society: Think about how you want to affect the world as a whole. How can you help solve social problems, promote justice, or speak up for causes that are important to you? How can you leave the world a better place?

To define your personal legacy, you need to think about your values, figure out the most important parts of your life, and be clear about the effect you want to have on your loved ones, your community, and society as a whole. By taking the time to think about yourself, you can make sure that your actions and decisions are in line with your ideals. This will have a lasting, positive effect on the people around you. Take advantage of the chance to live a life of purpose, authenticity, and important contributions that will inspire and uplift people for years to come.

Volunteering and Philanthropy

Volunteering and giving money to good causes are both strong ways to make the world a better place. This chapter talks about why it's important to give back, what volunteering and philanthropic work can do for people, and how to get involved in useful ways.

How to Figure Out What It Means

Giving Back: We can give back to our communities and make a change in the lives of others by volunteering and giving money. It gives us a chance to share our money, skills, and time to make the world a better place.

Change: By doing charity work and giving money to good causes, we can help solve social problems, bring about positive change, and improve the lives of people and communities in need.

Looking at the Options

Personal Values and Interests: Think about what you value and what you're interested in to find causes and groups that speak to you. Whether you're working on environmental protection, education, health care, or social justice, your efforts will be more meaningful if they are in line with your beliefs.

Local Community: Join community groups, non-profits, or charities in your area that work on problems you care about. Find out about volunteer options and what they are trying to do.

Giving your time, skills, and money

Volunteering: Give your time and energy to work that you don't get paid for. Think about what you're good at, what you're interested in, and when you're free to find chances that match your skills. Every act of service can make a difference, whether it's being a mentor or teacher, helping out at a food bank, or cleaning up your neighborhood.

Philanthropy is when you give money to nonprofits, charities, or organizations to help a good cause. Find groups that have a history of making good use of their resources and that share your goals. To make the biggest difference, you might want to make regular donations or take part in events to raise money.

Effects and Gains

Volunteering and giving money to good causes give people a sense of purpose and satisfaction. Knowing that your work makes a difference for the better can improve your general happiness and life satisfaction.

Volunteering and giving money help people get involved and connect with their communities. It lets you meet people who care about making a change as much as you do, so you can build relationships with people who share your passion.

Volunteering and giving money to good causes are great ways

to give back and make a difference in the world. You can help make change happen by looking for chances, making sure they fit with your values, and giving your time, skills, or money. Take pleasure in helping other people, and together we can make the world a better place for everyone.

Mentoring and Sharing Knowledge

Mentoring and sharing what you know are both strong ways to give back and help others. This chapter talks about the importance of mentoring, points out the benefits of sharing information, and gives advice on how to do these things well.

How to Figure Out What It Means

Mentoring is the process of giving advice, support, and knowledge to people who want to improve themselves or their careers. It lets people with a lot of experience share their knowledge and help younger people find their own ways to success.

Sharing information: Sharing information is the act of giving someone else your knowledge, skills, and ideas so they can use them. It helps people grow and develop as people, and it also helps society as a whole move forward.

Looking at the Options

Mentorship Programs: Take part in mentoring programs run by schools, professional groups, or neighborhood groups. These programs bring together mentors and mentees who want help in certain areas of interest or skill.

Offer to be a guide to people in your network or community who could learn from your experience and knowledge. Look for ways to meet people who are trying to get ahead and could use your help.

Effective mentoring and sharing of knowledge

Set up trust and rapport. Build a relationship with your mentee or audience built on trust and mutual respect. Make sure they feel safe and supported so they can talk about their goals, challenges, and ambitions.

Customize Your Approach: Figure out what your teacher or audience needs and wants, and then make sure your advice and knowledge sharing fits those needs and goals. Recognize that each person is different and adjust your way of teaching to meet their needs.

Offer Support and Encouragement: Give your mentee or audience support, encouragement, and helpful comments to help them grow and improve. Encourage them to reach their full potential by creating a setting that is positive and gives them power.

Share your resources and chances: Give them resources, tools, and growth chances to help them learn and grow. Give them suggestions for books, articles, classes, or networking events that can help them learn or improve.

The benefits and results

Personal Satisfaction: Being a mentor and sharing what you know can make you feel good. Seeing the growth and success of your mentees or the results of your efforts to share your knowledge can make you feel happy and proud.

Paying It Forward: By being a guide to others and sharing what you know, you help the next generation grow and develop. Your knowledge and experience can help people reach their goals and make a good difference in their own circles of influence.

Mentoring and sharing what you know are great ways to help others and make a difference in their lives. By participating in training programs, giving advice to people who want to get ahead, and sharing your knowledge in different ways, you can help others reach their full potential. Take advantage of the chance to share your knowledge and experiences, and together we can help create a culture of learning and growth that never stops.

Environmental Sustainability

In the world we live in now, environmental sustainability is more important than ever because of problems like climate change, pollution, and the loss of natural resources. This chapter talks about the importance of environmental sustainability, shows how each person can help protect the environment, and gives advice on how to adopt eco-friendly habits and support environmental projects.

How to Figure Out What It Means

Preservation of Ecosystems: The goal of environmental sustainability is to protect ecosystems and biodiversity, which helps keep the world and its people healthy and happy. It understands that human activities and the natural environment are connected and depend on each other.

Climate Change: Environmental sustainability handles the urgent need to fight climate change by reducing greenhouse gas emissions, switching to renewable energy sources, and adopting sustainable practices that reduce our ecological footprint.

Contributing to the preservation of the environment

Practices that are good for the environment: Do things like save energy and water, reduce waste, recycle, and use items that are good for the environment. Small things can add up to make a big difference when many people do them.

Sustainable Transportation: When you can, choose sustainable ways to get around, like walking, biking, or taking public transportation. To cut down on carbon pollution, you could carpool or buy electric cars.

Responsible Consumption: Choose products that are good for the earth, support local and sustainable businesses, and buy as few single-use items as possible. Choose wisely, putting sustainability and decent production methods at the top of your list.

Getting the word out about environmental stewardship

Raise awareness: Learn about environmental problems, their effects, and why it's important to use sustainable methods. Use social media to share information, take part in local events, or organize educational projects in your neighborhood.

Help Environmental Organizations: Donate to groups that work to protect the earth and keep it healthy. Donate your time, skills, or money to help them with their efforts to protect environments, fix up habitats, and encourage people to live in a way that is good for the environment.

Be an advocate for policy: Keep up with policies about the climate and work for responsible environmental stewardship on the local, national, and international levels. Write to lawmakers, take part in public meetings, and back projects that put sustainability first.

The benefits and results

Conservation of the environment: When you use sustainable methods and support environmental projects, you help protect natural resources, keep species safe, and keep ecosystems in good health.

Health and Well-Being: Practicing sustainability often leads to healthier surroundings and ways of life. Clean air, water, and less exposure to dangerous chemicals are good for the health of both people and other animals.

Future Generations: When we put environmental protection first, we make the world a better place for people who will come after us. What we do as a group today will affect how good life will be for those who come after us and what chances they will have.

For the environment to be sustainable, people, communities, companies, and governments all need to work together. We can make a positive difference on our world by doing things that are good for the environment, speaking up for responsible environmental stewardship, and giving money to groups that work to protect the environment. Let's try to take care of the environment in a reasonable way and work toward a future where the needs of the present can be met without making it harder for future generations to do the same.

Artistic Expression and Creativity

Creativity and artistic expression are powerful ways to show who you are, grow as a person, and leave a creative memory. This article talks about how important it is to be creative, shows different ways to be creative, and stresses how important it is to share your creative works with others.

Trying out artistic projects

Self-Expression: Artistic activities give people a unique way to share their ideas, feelings, and points of view. Artists can share their deepest thoughts and experiences through different forms of art, such as painting, writing, singing, or sculpture, which gives us a glimpse into their unique worldview.

Participating in arts activities can help you grow as a person and learn more about yourself. It gives people a chance to explore their imagination, try out new techniques, and learn new skills. Making art helps you think about yourself, figure out how to solve problems, and find your own artistic style.

Different ways to express art

Visual arts: Painting, drawing, photography, sculpting, and other visual arts allow people to show how they think, feel, and see the world. These kinds of art give people a way to express themselves in a tangible way and let people make works that are beautiful and make people feel different things.

Writing, poetry, and sharing stories are all examples of literary arts. Through writing, people can share their thoughts, stories, and experiences. With these ways of expressing art, language, images, and themes can be explored. This lets viewers go on imaginative journeys and connect with the writer's point of view.

The performing arts include music, dance, theater, and other forms of communication that are lively and passionate. Artists can make people feel things, tell stories, and connect with them on a deep level through music, movement, and theater performances, leaving a lasting impression through their work.

Sharing Creative Works

Exhibitions and performances: Artists can share their work with a bigger audience by putting it on display at exhibitions, concerts, dance performances, or theater productions. It lets the artist and the viewer talk to each other and share ideas, which builds a sense of connection and respect for artistic expression.

Publications and digital platforms: Artists can reach a wider audience and make a lasting effect by publishing written works, putting out music albums, or sharing visual art through books, magazines, online platforms, or social media. These platforms give artists and art lovers the chance to work together, get comments, and talk with each other.

Engaging with the community through workshops, art classes, or public art projects makes room for teamwork, mentoring, and the sharing of artistic knowledge. It helps people feel like they are part of a group and gives artists a chance to inspire and encourage other people to explore their own creativity.

Creative expression and artistic expression are important for personal growth, self-expression, and leaving a creative legacy. Participating in the creative arts, literary arts, or performing arts is a way to learn about yourself, discover new things, and connect with other people. Artists can have a long effect on people and society as a whole by sharing their work through exhibitions, performances, publications, and involvement in the community. Let's use art as a way to honor the human spirit, spark people's imaginations, and encourage them to find their own creative potential.

Inspiring Future Generations

A strong way to change the world for the better is to inspire and give power to younger people. This chapter talks about how important it is to spend time with younger people, the role of mentoring, and how important it is to encourage people to have a growth mindset, be resilient, and follow their interests.

Getting in touch with younger people

Connection is important because it helps you make real connections with younger people and gives you both chances to grow and learn. It helps people of different ages understand each other and builds a sense of community and support.

Sharing Life Experiences: Telling younger people about your successes and failures can give them useful advice and help them learn from your mistakes. By talking about their own experiences, lessons they've learned, and how they overcame problems, mentors can inspire and support young people to go through their own lives with confidence and strength.

What a mentor does

Mentoring gives advice, support, and encouragement to younger people as they go through different parts of life, such as school, job choices, and personal growth. Mentors can help by giving advice, giving different points of view, and giving drive and inspiration.

Empowering Through Role Models: Mentors serve as good role models, showing what is possible and how to be successful. Mentors encourage younger people to believe in themselves and go after their dreams by talking about their own successes and showing them how to be persistent, determined, and honest.

Getting people to think about growth and passion

Accepting a Growth Mindset: Helping younger people build a growth mindset helps them believe in their ability to learn, grow, and deal with problems. It teaches people to be strong, flexible, and open to new chances for personal and professional growth.

Pursuing Passions: Helping young people develop a passion-driven mindset gives them the freedom to explore their interests, skills, and special strengths. When you encourage them to do what they love, you give them energy, spark their creativity, and give them a feeling of purpose and satisfaction in their lives.

Inspiring and enabling the next generation is a good thing to do that can make the future better for everyone and for society as a whole. By talking to younger people, sharing our own life experiences, and being a guide, we can help them make good decisions, get past problems, and reach their full potential. By encouraging them to have a growth mindset, be resilient, and follow their passions, we encourage them to use their unique skills to make a difference in the world. Let's work together to motivate and inspire the next generation, leaving behind a legacy of success, kindness, and new ideas.

Documenting Your Life Story

Writing down your life story is a strong way to make sure that your experiences, wisdom, and personal journey will be remembered by people in the future. This article talks about how important it is to keep track of your life story, how writing a memoir or journal can help, and how there are different ways to share your story with other people.

How to Keep Your Story

Legacy and Family History: Writing down your life story makes sure that your unique experiences and family history are passed down to future generations. It helps your descendants understand where they came from, their cultural background, and the struggles and successes that shaped the story of their family.

Lessons and Insights: Your life story is full of lessons, insights, and wisdom that you've learned through your own situations. By writing down these lessons, you give future generations advice and motivation. You also give them a different point of view that can help them get through their own lives with more understanding and strength.

How to Write a Journal or Memoir

Self-Reflection and Self-Discovery: Writing a diary or journal gives you a chance to think about yourself and learn more about yourself. It gives you a chance to think about your thoughts, feelings, and the big moments that changed your life. You learn more about yourself and the trip you're on as you go through this process.

Keeping Track of Important Milestones: A memoir or journal can help you keep track of important events, accomplishments, difficulties, and how you grew as a person along the way. It shows how strong you are, what you've done, and the important things you've learned in your life.

Telling the story of your life

Family and Loved Ones: Telling your life story to family and friends helps people from different groups connect and understand each other better. It makes family ties stronger, gives people a sense of belonging, and gets people talking about their shared experiences and beliefs.

Storytelling Platforms and Publications: With the rise of technology, there are now many ways to tell your life story to a bigger audience. Blogs, social media, and platforms for self-publishing give you the chance to tell your story, inspire others, and leave a lasting legacy that goes beyond your immediate group.

Documenting your life story is an important thing to do because it lets you keep your experiences, knowledge, and personal journey alive for future generations. By writing a biography or a journal, you can look back on your life, remember important moments, and teach others important lessons. Your life story has the power to inspire, teach, and connect people across time and space, whether you tell it to your family or on a speaking platform. Seize the chance to write down your life story and leave a lasting memory that future generations will treasure.

Advocacy and Social Change

Advocacy and social change are both strong ways to change the world for the better. This chapter talks about the importance of advocacy, the role of raising awareness, and the different things people can do to help bring about good social change.

Why it's Important to Advocate

Giving Voice to the Voiceless: Advocacy gives people or groups whose views might not be heard otherwise a chance to be heard. By standing up for causes and speaking out, we can make sure that the concerns and needs of disadvantaged or vulnerable groups are heard, which is good for both social justice and inclusion.

Awareness: Advocacy is a very important way to make people aware of different social, environmental, or human rights problems. It helps teach the public, dispel myths, and build empathy, all of which are important for building a society that is more compassionate and well-informed.

Using Your Voice to Make a Difference

Find the Causes: The first step in advocacy is to find causes and problems that fit with your values and your own life. Choose a cause that you care about and that fits with your values. It could be about human rights, the environment, gender equality, or education.

Raising knowledge is one of the most important parts of advocacy. This can be done in many ways, such as by giving speeches, running campaigns on social media, writing articles, or putting on community events. By telling people facts, stories, and your point of view, you can start important conversations and motivate them to act.

How to Be Part of Social Change

Community Organizations: If you join a community organization or a non-profit group that works on a specific cause, you can work with other people who share your interests to reach a shared goal. Most of the time, these groups offer chances to volunteer, plan events, and work for change at the local level.

Grassroots movements: These are strong ways to bring about social change. They bring together people who care about a certain cause and want to make a difference by working together, raising awareness, and advocating. By joining grassroots groups, you can help create a groundswell of support and speed up the process of change.

Political Advocacy: Influencing lawmakers and legislative processes to bring about systemic change is what political advocacy is all about. This can be done by lobbying, getting in touch with elected officials, or joining campaigns and movements that push for policy changes that are in line with your cause.

People have the chance to make a difference in the world through advocacy and social change. We can help change society for the better by speaking up for causes that are important to us, raising awareness, and getting active in community groups or grassroots movements. Remember that even small acts can have a big impact, and that together we can make a more fair, just, and long-lasting future for everyone. Advocacy is a powerful tool that can lead to good changes in your community and beyond.

Fostering Meaningful Relationships

To live a full and connected life, it's important to build meaningful connections. This article talks about how important it is to put relationships first, take care of family ties and friendships, and build a support system that helps us stick to our values and goals.

Why meaningful relationships are important

Emotional Well-Being: Our overall emotional well-being is helped by having meaningful connections. They give us support, love, and a feeling that we belong, all of which are important to our mental and emotional health. Relationships that are good can help you feel less stressed, happier, and give you a sense of purpose and satisfaction.

Social Support: When things are hard, having strong relationships can help. They help us feel better, give us hope, and listen to us when we need it most. Having ties to family, friends, or the community gives us a sense of comfort and helps us get through the ups and downs of life.

Taking care of family ties

Quality Time: Spending quality time with family members makes the ties stronger and creates memories that will last a lifetime. Make it a priority to do things with your family on a daily basis, eat together, and talk about important things to get closer.

Communication and Understanding: For family ties to grow,

there needs to be good communication and active listening. Encourage people to talk to each other in an open and honest way and to fix problems with empathy and understanding.

How to Make Good Friends

Shared Interests and Activities: People often become close friends when they do things they both like and enjoy. Participate in sports or join groups and communities that are related to your interests. This will give you the chance to meet people who share your interests and help you make deep connections with them.

Support and Empathy: Support and empathy are two things that make friends stronger. Be there for your friends when they are happy and when they are having a hard time. Listen to them and enjoy their successes. Build your friendships on faith and giving and taking.

Putting together a support system

Community Engagement: Getting involved in your community gives you chances to meet people who share your values and goals. Get active in community groups, events, or volunteer work to meet people who share your values and build a network of people who agree with you.

Mentorship and Guidance: Be a mentor and guide to younger people or people who could learn from your experience and knowledge. By helping others and sharing what you know, you can make important connections and help other people grow.

Building meaningful connections is a lifelong process that takes thought, time, and work. By putting family and friends first, making strong friendships, and creating a network of support, we can make deep connections and leave a lasting mark. Meaningful ties are good for our health, help us through hard times, and make us feel like we belong. Recognize how important relationships are, put time and effort into making them better, and enjoy the wealth and satisfaction they bring to your life.

By consciously shaping your legacy and leaving a positive impact, you can create a lasting imprint that extends beyond your retirement years. In the next chapter, we will address the top 30 questions most people ask about retirement and provide comprehensive answers.

Get ready to gain valuable insights and clarity in Chapter 8: Frequently Asked Questions about Retirement.

9

Frequently Asked Questions about Retirement

Chapter 8 aims to address the top 30 questions that most people have about retirement. These questions cover a wide range of topics and provide comprehensive answers to help you navigate the complexities of planning for and enjoying your retirement years.

When should you start making plans for retirement?
The best time to plan for retirement is as soon as possible, so that your cash and investments can grow as much as possible.

How much do I need to save to be able to retire?
How much money you need to save for retirement depends on how you want to live, how much you spend, and how long you plan to live. The best way to get a personalized quote is to talk to a financial advisor.

What are the different ways to save for retirement?

401(k) plans, IRAs (both traditional and Roth), pension plans, annuities, and taxed investment accounts are all ways to save for retirement.

Should I put money into an IRA, a 401(k), or both?

Whether you put money into a 401(k), an IRA, or both relies on whether you are eligible, whether your employer matches your contributions, and what tax benefits each account type has.

How do I figure out how much I'll get from Social Security?

You can figure out how much your Social Security payments will be based on how much money you've made in the past and how old you are when you decide to start getting them. Estimates can be made by the Social Security Administration.

How can I get the most out of my investments so I can retire?

Most of the time, the best way to spend for retirement is to build a balanced, diversified portfolio that fits your risk tolerance, time horizon, and financial goals. Getting help from a professional can be helpful.

How can I make sure that my retirement savings will last my whole life?

To make sure your retirement savings last, you can do things like set a reasonable withdrawal rate, change your spending based on how the market is doing, and think about annuities or other products that give you a steady stream of income.

Should I think about getting insurance for long-term care?

Long-term care insurance is something to think about if you want to protect yourself from the high costs of long-term health care in retirement.

How does income from retirement affect taxes?

Depending on where the money comes from (e.g., Social Security, pensions, or withdrawals from retirement accounts), the tax consequences of retirement income can be different. For specific advice, talk to a tax expert.

How do I choose the best health insurance for when I retire?

When you retire, choosing the right health insurance means weighing your needs and budget against choices like Medicare, supplemental insurance plans (Medigap), and Medicare Advantage plans.

Can I keep working when I'm retired?

You can work after you retire, but it relies on your situation, your financial goals, and your personal preferences. Part-time work or following a hobby can help retirees make more money.

What are the pros and cons of moving into less space when you retire?

When you retire, downsizing can help you save money on expenses and maintenance, but it's important to think about things like location, changes in your lifestyle, and your emotional attachment to your present home.

How do I make a retirement budget?

To make a budget for retirement, you need to look at your expected income, spending, and financial goals. Think about all of your sources of income and plan for both necessary and optional costs.

What should you think about if you want to move after you retire?

When deciding where to move after retirement, you should think about things like the cost of living, the weather, how close you will be to family and friends, and how easy it will be to get to the services and activities you want.

How do I handle bills in retirement?

Taking care of debt in retirement is important to keep money worries to a minimum. Pay off debts with high interest rates first and think about refinancing, consolidating debt, or working with a financial advisor.

Should I pay off my home before I retire?

Paying off your mortgage before you retire can give you peace of mind and lower your monthly costs, but it depends on your finances and other things. Check out the interest rates, the tax effects, and the cash flow.

What are the best ways to cut costs when you retire?

You can cut costs in retirement by reviewing your budget, figuring out which costs aren't necessary, downsizing your living situation, looking for deals, and being careful about spending you don't have to.

How should I plan for inflation when I retire?

Planning for inflation in retirement means thinking about investment strategies that try to beat inflation, making changes to your retirement budget over time, and maybe even buying assets that protect you from inflation.

What ways are there to make money after you retire?

There are many ways to make money in retirement, such as through investments, Social Security, pensions, part-time work, annuities, and gains from stocks or bonds.

Do you really need a financial advisor when you retire?

Even though it's not necessary, a financial adviser can help retirees make good decisions about investments, taxes, withdrawals, estate planning, and managing their money in general.

How can I keep my retirement savings safe from changes in the market?

Diversifying investments, thinking about conservative asset allocation, using methods like dollar-cost averaging, and keeping your mind on long-term goals are all ways to protect your retirement savings from market volatility.

What are the best ways to plan your estate when you retire?

When you retire, you need to make or update a will, think about trusts, name beneficiaries, and work with legal and financial pros to make sure your assets are given to the people you want.

Can I travel and do things I enjoy after I retire without using up all my savings?

Traveling and doing hobbies in retirement can be done without using up all your savings if you plan ahead, look for cheap choices, and carefully manage your money.

How do I keep myself busy and social after I retire?

Volunteering, joining clubs or organizations, pursuing hobbies, taking part in community events, and staying in touch with family and friends are all ways to stay socially involved and engaged after retirement.

What should you think about when making a healthcare proxy or an advance directive?

Healthcare proxies and advance instructions are important things to think about when you retire to make sure that your healthcare decisions are made according to your wishes if you are unable to do so.

Should I think about retiring in stages?

The shift from full-time work to retirement can be made gradually with a phased retirement plan. This could reduce the financial and emotional impact of retirement and provide extra income during the transition period.

How do I pay for unexpected costs when I'm retired?

When you retire, you can deal with unexpected costs by keeping an emergency fund, getting enough insurance, and adjusting your budget or investment strategy as required.

How can I get money out of my retirement account before

I'm 59 12?

Some exceptions to early exit penalties for certain retirement accounts, loans from 401(k) plans, or substantially equal periodic payments (SEPP) under IRS rules are all ways to get to retirement funds before age 59 12.

How do I figure out Medicare and extra insurance, which are both complicated?

To figure out how to use Medicare and supplemental insurance, you need to know about enrollment periods, coverage choices, premiums, and coverage gaps. Medicare advisers can be helpful when it comes to research, consultations, and giving advice.

How can I make sure my loved ones have money after I'm gone?

You can leave a financial legacy for your loved ones by planning your estate, setting up trusts, naming heirs, thinking about life insurance, and working with professionals to make sure your assets are distributed correctly.

By addressing these commonly asked questions, you can gain clarity and confidence in your retirement planning journey.

In the final chapter, we will summarize the key takeaways from the book and provide a tool to help you create a roadmap for your successful retirement journey.

Get ready to embark on the path to a remarkable retirement

in Chapter 9: The Roadmap to Retirement Success.

10

The Roadmap to Retirement Success

This chapter serves as a roadmap to guide you towards a successful and fulfilling retirement. It consolidates the key takeaways from the book and provides a step-by-step approach to help you navigate the various aspects of retirement planning and living. Let's explore the essential elements of a successful retirement and outline the path to achieving your retirement goals.

Define Your Retirement Vision

Having a clear idea of what you want your retirement to look like is an important step in getting ready for a happy and successful retirement. This chapter talks about how to think about your ideal living, set goals, and come up with a plan that fits with your goals for retirement.

Thinking About the Life You Want

Think about your lifestyle: Start by thinking about how you want to live when you quit. Think about things like where you want to live, how you will move, what you like to do for fun, and who you know. Think about how you'd like to spend your time and what makes you happy and satisfied.

Health and Happiness: Put your health and well-being at the top of your retirement plans. Think about how you want to take care of your physical and mental health, exercise regularly, do things you enjoy, and put yourself first. Think about what tools and support you might need to live a healthy life.

Making plans

SMART Goals: Set specific, measurable, achievable, relevant, and time-bound (SMART) goals to guide your picture of retirement. You could set goals like becoming financially independent, planning trips, learning new skills or hobbies, giving back through charity work, or spending quality time with people you care about.

Prioritizing Goals: Think about how important and possible each goal is in light of your values and goals. Focus your efforts on the goals that are most in line with how you want to spend your retirement.

Making a plan for retirement

Create a clear picture in your mind of what a happy retirement looks like to you. Think about the things, people, and events that make you the happiest and most fulfilled. Visualize yourself living out your retirement goal.

Write It Down: Put your plans for retirement in writing or on a vision board. Give a detailed account of what you want to do and see during your retired years. Be clear about the kind of life you want to live and the goals you want to reach.

Defining your retirement vision is a process that gives you power and helps you make a plan for a successful and enjoyable retirement. By thinking about the kind of life you want, setting SMART goals, and making a clear vision, you can make sure that your actions and choices are in line with what you want. Review your plan for retirement often and make changes as needed, so that it can change along with your life and hobbies. If you have a clear plan for your retirement years, you can go into them with purpose, desire, and a clear sense of direction.

Assess Your Financial Readiness

A key part of getting ready for a safe and happy retirement is figuring out how financially stable you are. This chapter looks at how to evaluate your current financial position, figure out how much money you'll need in retirement, and get professional help to make the most of your retirement savings and investments.

Think about how your money is going right now

Income and Expenses: Figure out how much you make and how much you spend each month. Think about your salary, investments, rent, and any other cash you get. Look at how you spend your money and find places where you can cut back to save more.

Debts and liabilities: Take a look at your mortgages, loans, and credit card amounts to see how much you still owe. Make a plan to pay off high-interest debts and cut down on financial responsibilities before you retire to make your finances easier.

Determine Your Retirement Income Needs

Retirement Lifestyle: Determine the lifestyle you imagine for your retirement years. Think about things like living, travel, health care, hobbies, and helping people who depend on you. Figure out how much it will cost to live the way you want to live.

Sources of Income: List the possible sources of income in retirement, such as pensions, Social Security payouts, retirement savings, and income from investments. Calculate how much money you expect to get from each source and decide if it will be enough to meet your income needs in retirement.

Calculate Your Retirement Savings

Retirement Savings Evaluation: Figure out how much your individual retirement accounts (IRAs), 401(k) plans, and other investment accounts are worth right now. Think about how fast your investments will grow and how much you might get back from them.

Retirement Savings Gap: Compare how much you think you will need to live on in retirement with how much you think you will have saved. Find out if there is a deficit or a profit. If there is a gap, look into ways to save more or make changes to your retirement plans.

Get help from a professional

Talk to a Financial Advisor: Hire a qualified financial advisor who specializes in helping people plan for retirement. They can give you expert advice, look at your finances, and help you make an individualized plan for retirement.

Work with your financial advisor to make sure your retirement plans and investments are the best they can be. They can suggest good ways to spend, diversify your portfolio, and change your asset allocation based on how much risk you are willing to take and what your financial goals are.

To have a safe and happy future, you need to figure out how financially ready you are for retirement. By looking at your current financial position, figuring out how much money you'll need in retirement, and getting advice from a professional, you can make smart decisions and take the steps you need to make the most of your retirement savings and investments. Review and change your financial plan often as your life changes to make sure you have enough money for retirement. You can start your retirement with confidence and peace of mind if you plan it well and get help from experts.

Develop a Retirement Income Strategy

Making a complete plan for your retirement income is important if you want to be financially secure and live the way you want to when you leave. This chapter explains the main steps you need to take to make a plan for your retirement income, such as finding possible sources of income, making a budget, and looking into ways to make the most of your retirement income.

Find Possible Ways to Make Money in Retirement

Pensions: Check to see if your workplace or any other pension plans will give you a pension. Learn about the terms and conditions of your pension and estimate how much money it will give you when you leave.

Social Security: Figure out if you are eligible and learn about the perks offered by the Social Security Administration. Think about things like the best age to start getting benefits and any possible cuts or increases based on when you want to retire.

Investments: Look at your portfolio of investments and think about how much money it might bring in when you leave. Think about sources like individual retirement accounts (IRAs), 401(k) plans, pensions, stock dividends, and bond interest.

Create a Budget

Lifestyle Assessment: Determine your ideal lifestyle during retirement. Think about things like housing, health care, travel, sports, and other costs that are specific to you. Be reasonable and think about both necessary and optional costs.

Income and Expense Analysis: Look at how much you expect to get from pensions, Social Security, and assets in retirement and how much you expect to spend. Make sure that your pay is enough to cover all of your costs. If you don't have enough money, look for ways to make more money or reduce your spending.

Explore Strategies to Maximize Retirement Income

Putting Off Social Security Benefits: You might want to put off getting your Social Security benefits until after the age for early retirement. If you wait until your full retirement age or even later, you can get higher monthly benefits, which will give you a bigger stream of income during retirement.

Part-Time Work: Think about the idea of working part-time after you quit. This can help you make more money while keeping you busy and active. Think about using your skills and knowledge in an open way or looking for new opportunities that fit with what you're interested in.

Work with a financial expert to make sure that your retirement investments are the best they can be. Change the way you divide up your assets, diversify your portfolio, and look into low-risk ways to make steady income. Review and adjust your investments often based on how the market is doing and how your financial goals change.

Creating a plan for your retirement income is important if you want to be financially secure and live the way you want to in your golden years. You can feel positive about your retirement years if you find possible sources of income, make a budget that fits your lifestyle, and look into ways to make the most of your retirement income. Review and change your plan for getting money in retirement often as things change to make sure it still fits with your goals. You can have a happy and financially safe retirement if you plan well and make decisions ahead of time.

Plan for Healthcare and Long-Term Care

Planning for long-term care and health care is an important part of getting ready for retirement. This chapter talks about the steps you need to take to make a complete plan for health care and long-term care, such as studying your options, learning about costs, thinking about insurance, and making a plan for how to handle things.

Check out your options and costs for health care

Medicare: Learn about the different parts (Part A, Part B, Part C, and Part D) and what they cover. Find out what you need to do to be eligible and how to sign up. Find out how much your Medicare rates, deductibles, and copayments will cost.

Supplemental Insurance: You might want to buy extra insurance, like Medigap plans, to pay for costs that Medicare doesn't cover. Look into different insurance companies and plans to find the one that meets your wants and fits your budget the best.

Long-Term Care: Look into nursing homes, assisted living facilities, and home healthcare as choices for long-term care and their costs. Find out what you need to do to apply for long-term care services and how much it might cost. Think about the benefits of long-term care insurance if you want to protect yourself against high medical costs in the future.

Think about insurance for long-term care

Evaluate Your Needs: Look at your health history, the health history of your family, and your finances to see if long-term care insurance is right for you. Think about your age, your current health, the help of your family, and the cost of long-term care.

Check out insurance companies: Find out about the different companies that offer long-term care insurance and what they cover. Compare plans, choices for coverage, costs, and benefits. Think about things like protection against inflation, elimination periods, and coverage limits to find the best insurance for your needs.

Talk to a Financial Advisor: Talk to a financial advisor who specializes in planning for retirement and long-term care insurance. They can give you advice that is tailored to your situation and help you make an informed choice about long-term care insurance.

Make a plan for healthcare and long-term care management

Review Your Plan Often: Look over your health plan, including Medicare and any extra insurance, on a regular basis. Stay up to date on any changes to Medicare policies and benefits that could affect your costs and needs for health care.

Build a network of healthcare providers by doing research and getting to know those who specialize in senior care or have experience with retirement and long-term care needs. Choose health care providers who fit with your tastes and can meet your needs.

Talk to your family: Talk to your family members or chosen caregivers about your plan for long-term care and health care. Make sure they know what you want and understand your choices about your health care.

Planning for healthcare and long-term care is important if you want a smooth move into retirement and to protect yourself from possible healthcare costs. By learning about your health care choices and costs, thinking about long-term care insurance, and making a plan, you can be better prepared to handle your health care needs and possible long-term care needs. Review and change your plan often as your situation changes, and talk to experts for personalized advice. With an all-inclusive plan for health care and long-term care, you can relax and focus on having a healthy and rewarding retirement.

Establish an Estate Plan

Setting up an estate plan is one of the most important things you can do to make sure that your assets are handled and given away according to your wishes after you die. This chapter talks about the most important parts of an estate plan, such as talking to an attorney, making legal papers, naming beneficiaries, thinking about tax-efficient strategies, and reviewing the plan on a regular basis.

Talk to an attorney about estate planning

Get help from a professional. Hire an experienced estate planning lawyer who can give you advice based on your unique situation and help you handle the legal complexities of estate planning. They will help you understand the different choices you have and make sure your plan follows the laws.

Make a will or update it. A will is one of the most important documents in estate planning. Work with your lawyer to make a complete will that spells out how you want your assets to be divided, who will take care of your young children (if you have any), and who will be in charge of carrying out your wishes.

Think about trusts and other legal documents. Depending

on how complicated your estate is and what your goals are, your lawyer may suggest setting up trusts, such as revocable living trusts or irrevocable trusts, to give you more control and flexibility over how your assets are managed and to reduce the need for probate.

Choose the people who will benefit and plan for tax efficiency

Identify Beneficiaries: Make sure your bank accounts, retirement accounts, life insurance plans, and investment accounts have clear beneficiaries. Review and update your beneficiary choices on a regular basis to make sure they still reflect what you want.

Tax-Efficient Strategies: Discuss tax-efficient ways to pass on your wealth with your estate planning lawyer and tax expert. This could mean taking advantage of exemptions and deductions, setting up charity trusts, or making gifts during your lifetime to lower your estate tax liability.

Coordinate with Other Professionals: Work with your financial advisor, accountant, and other professionals to make sure your estate plan fits in with your general financial strategy and gets you the most tax benefits.

Review and keep your will up to date

Periodic Review: You should look over your estate plan on a regular basis to make sure it keeps up with any changes in your life, such as marriage, divorce, births, deaths, or big changes in your finances. Make sure your plan matches your present goals and wishes.

Talk to Your Loved Ones: Tell your loved ones, like family members and the people you've chosen as receivers, about your estate plan. Give them information and directions about your plan to keep them from getting confused and causing problems in the future.

Talk to Your Lawyer: Set up regular meetings with your lawyer who helps you plan your estate to review and update your plan as needed. They can help you deal with any changes in the law or in your tastes and make sure your plan is always up to date.

Setting up an estate plan is one of the most important things you can do to protect your memory and make sure your assets are distributed the way you want. You can be sure that your estate will be handled according to your wishes if you talk to an estate planning lawyer, make or update a will and other legal documents, name beneficiaries, think about tax-saving strategies, and review your plan on a regular basis. Don't forget to talk to professionals, tell your loved ones about your plan, and change it as your life changes. With a well-thought-out estate plan, you can take care of your family, avoid fights, and leave a lasting memory.

Embrace Lifestyle Choices

When you retire, you have the chance to make lifestyle choices that fit with your interests, morals, and personal tastes. This chapter talks about how important it is to figure out how you want to spend your time in retirement, do things that make you happy and fulfilled, keep up with friends and hobbies, and find a good mix between leisure, work, and personal growth.

Think about how you'd like to spend your time

Think About Your hobbies: Give yourself time to think about your hobbies, values, and goals. Think about the things you've done in your life that have made you happy and fulfilled, and plan out how you'd like to spend your time when you leave.

Set Goals and Priorities: Make sure your retired lifestyle has clear goals and priorities. Define what's most important to you, whether it's traveling, learning a new skill, helping, or spending quality time with loved ones, and make a plan for how to get there.

Do things that bring you joy and satisfaction

Pursue your hobbies and interests: Do things that you love and that make you happy. Immerse yourself in activities that feed your soul and make you feel like you've accomplished something, like drawing, playing an instrument, gardening, or playing sports.

Explore New Interests: Take advantage of the chance to try out new skills and interests. People can try new things, learn new skills, and find hidden abilities when they retire. Lifelong learning and joining clubs and organizations can help you meet new people and learn about new things.

Foster connections and relationships with other people

Relationships should be a top priority. Spend time building and maintaining meaningful relationships with family, friends, and coworkers. Keep in touch regularly, take part in social activities, and make sure you have chances to do things together that will help you get closer and build memories that will last.

Join Community Groups and Organizations: Join community groups, clubs, or organizations that match your hobbies. This can lead to social contacts, networking, and sharing experiences with people who have similar interests.

Find a Good Middle Ground

Leisure and Relaxation: Do things for fun that help you relax, recharge, and relieve stress. Take care of yourself, do things you enjoy, and enjoy the easy things in life.

Productivity and Personal Growth: Look for ways to improve yourself and get things done. Think about doing part-time work, starting a small business, or doing volunteer work in an area that fits your skills and hobbies. This can give you a sense of purpose, keep your mind active, and make you feel like you're still making a difference.

When you retire, you can start a new part of your life where you can make choices that bring you happiness, satisfaction, and a sense of meaning. By planning how you want to spend your time, doing things that make you happy, staying in touch with friends and family, and finding a good balance between leisure, work, and personal growth, you can create a fulfilling and meaningful retirement lifestyle for yourself. Enjoy the freedom to explore your interests, connect with other people, and do things that are good for your general health. Retirement can be a time of self-discovery, personal growth, and deep happiness if you choose your lifestyle wisely.

Prioritize Health and Wellness

Putting health and fitness first is important if you want to live a full and happy life, especially in retirement. This article shows how important it is to put your health first by living a healthy lifestyle, going to the doctor regularly, and doing things that help your mental and emotional health.

Choosing a healthy way of life

Regular Exercise: Be active regularly to improve your health and well-being as a whole. Pick things you like to do, like walking, swimming, yoga, or riding. Aim for a mix of cardio, strength training, and flexibility workouts to keep your body fit and mobile.

Diet that is good for you: Try to eat a healthy, well-balanced diet with a range of fruits, vegetables, whole grains, lean proteins, and healthy fats. Don't eat too much prepared food, sugary drinks, or salt and sugar. Drink enough water throughout the day to keep yourself refreshed.

Setting up regular doctor visits and preventive care: Regular Health Check-ups: Set up regular medical check-ups with your doctor to keep an eye on your general health, talk about any possible health problems, and get any screenings or vaccinations you need. This proactive method lets any health problems be found and treated quickly.

Preventive Care Measures: Stay up-to-date on preventive care measures like tests for cancer, cholesterol levels, blood pressure, and vaccinations. Follow the guidelines for your age, gender, and health history to lower your chance of getting a long-term illness.

Adding Activities for Mental and Emotional Health

Mindfulness and Stress Management: Practice mindfulness methods like meditation, deep breathing exercises, or yoga to reduce stress and improve mental health. Do things that help you calm down and relax, like reading, listening to music, or spending time in nature.

Self-care: Give the most importance to self-care tasks that improve your emotional health. This could mean doing things you enjoy, taking time for yourself, being kind to yourself, and getting help when you need it from doctors or support groups. Find things to do that make you happy, give you energy, and help you keep a good attitude.

Putting health and wellness first is important if you want to have a happy and successful retirement. You can improve your general quality of life by living a healthy lifestyle, getting regular medical checkups, and doing things that help your mental and emotional health. Remember that taking small steps every day can make a big difference in your health and well-being. Embrace the power of self-care and make your health a top concern. This will help you get the most out of retirement and all of its benefits and experiences.

Stay Engaged and Connected

Especially in retirement, staying active and connected to other people is important for a satisfying and purposeful life. This chapter talks about how important it is to have real relationships, do social things, and stay informed in order to feel connected and satisfied.

Build Relationships That Matter

Family and Friends: Make it a priority to care for and improve your ties with your family and close friends. Spend valuable time together, talk to each other often, and make memories that will last. Do things that bring you closer together and help you understand each other, like sharing meals, trips, or holidays.

Community Involvement: Get involved in your community by going to local events, joining clubs or groups, or giving your time to issues that interest you. Getting involved with people who have the same interests and values as you can help you feel like you fit and have a purpose.

Do things with other people

Socializing: Look for ways to meet new people and take part in activities that bring people closer together. Go to gatherings, parties, or events in your neighborhood. Join a club for your hobby, a book club, or a sports team to meet new people and make more friends.

Work as a volunteer: Look into volunteer options that match your skills and interests. Giving your time and skills to important causes helps other people and gives you a feeling of fulfillment and purpose. It can also help people meet new people and make new friends in the neighborhood.

Keep up with news and get involved

Current Events: Keep up with news, current events, and themes that interest you, both locally and around the world. Read newspapers, keep up with reputable news sources, or join online talks to learn more and see things from different points of view. Having deep talks with other people can help you learn more and make more intellectual connections.

Lifelong Learning: Keep a curious and open mind by learning new things throughout your life. Go to seminars, workshops, or internet classes on topics that interest you. Continuous learning not only helps you keep your mind sharp, but it also gives you chances to meet people who share your intellectual interest.

For a fulfilling retirement, it's important to stay busy and linked. You can develop a sense of belonging, purpose, and satisfaction by having meaningful relationships with family, friends, and people in your community, taking part in social activities, and staying informed and involved. Take advantage of chances to connect with people, do things that make you happy, and stay interested in the world around you. Remember that the people you meet and the things you do together can make your life better and help you have a full and happy retirement.

Adapt and Adjust

Retirement is a changing time of life, so it's important to be open to changing and adapting your plan as things change. This chapter shows how important it is to keep looking at your retiring goals, making changes as needed, and getting help and advice when you need it.

Continuous Evaluation

Assess your work toward your retirement goals on a regular basis. Review your finances, the way you want to live, and your personal goals to make sure they still fit with your original plan. Think about things like how the market is doing, how your health needs are changing, or how your family is doing.

Rethinking Goals: As retirement goes on, your goals and objectives may change. Take the time to think about what's most important to you at different points in your retirement. This could mean reevaluating your financial goals, lifestyle choices, or goals for personal satisfaction to make sure they still fit with your current situation and goals.

Making the Needed Changes

Adaptations: Keep an eye on how your finances are changing and make changes to your retirement plan as needed. This could mean changing the way you save or trade, looking for other ways to make money, or changing your budget to account for unexpected costs or changes in your lifestyle.

Lifestyle Flexibility: Be willing to change how you live in retirement as your needs change. Think about whether shrinking, moving, or starting new hobbies or activities fits with your changing interests and finances. Being flexible can help you deal with things you didn't plan for or take advantage of new possibilities.

Looking for Help and Direction

Professional Advice: To get help from a professional, talk to financial advisors, retirement managers, or lawyers who specialize in estate planning. They can help you make difficult financial choices, give you objective advice, and suggest changes that are in line with your goals and how much risk you are willing to take.

Support Networks: Join support groups, communities for seniors, or organizations that help older people. These networks can help you deal with the challenges and changes that come with retirement by giving you access to useful tools, peer support, and shared experiences.

Changing and adapting your retirement plan is a normal and important part of the road to retirement. By checking in on your progress often, making changes as needed, and asking for help and advice, you can make sure that your retirement is still satisfying and fits your changing needs and goals. Accept that you can change your cash plans, the way you live, and your personal goals as needed. Don't forget that asking for help and making connections with people who have had similar experiences can give you important insights and help during your retirement. Stay on the ball, be open to change, and take advantage of the chances that come your way.

By following this plan, you can easily deal with the many challenges of retirement and build a life that gives you a sense of purpose, makes you happy, and gives you financial security. Congratulations on starting this exciting trip to a great retirement! May your retirement years be full of joy, happiness, and a lot of options.

11

Conclusion

In this book, we looked at the new retirement plan, which goes beyond financial comfort and includes all of the things that make a life full and meaningful. We've talked about everything from financial planning and investing to health and fitness, leaving a legacy, and making the most of your retirement.

Don't forget that retirement is a personal journey, and there is no one way to do it. Use the ideas and techniques in this book as a starting point and change them to fit your own needs and goals. Take advantage of the chances that come with retirement and enjoy this new part of your life.

As you start your journey into retirement, surround yourself with a support network of professionals, loved ones, and people with similar interests who can help guide you, cheer you on, and keep you company. Stay interested, stay active, and enjoy the excitement that comes with retirement. Work through the action plan worksheet provided to start putting your plan together today!

We wish you a wonderful retirement with lots of joy, fulfillment, and opportunities to live your best life.

12

Retirement Action Plan Worksheet

1. The Shift in Retirement Paradigm:

- Research and understand why traditional retirement plans are no longer effective and why a new approach is necessary.
- _____
  ____ (Specific action to take)
- _____
  ____ (Specific action to take)

1. The Mindset of Financial Freedom:

- Reflect on your current mindset towards money and retirement.
- Identify any limiting beliefs or fears that may hinder your financial independence.
- _____
  ____ (Specific action to take)

- _____
  ____ (Specific action to take)

1. Unleashing Your True Potential:

- Assess your unique skills, talents, and passions.
- Brainstorm ways to incorporate them into your retirement plan.
- _____
  ___ (Specific action to take)
- _____
  ___ (Specific action to take)

1. Income Generation Strategies:

- Research and explore different income-generating opportunities during retirement, such as passive income streams or entrepreneurship.
- _____
  ____ (Specific action to take)
- _____
  ____ (Specific action to take)

1. Smart Investment Principles:

- Educate yourself on intelligent investing principles.
- Seek professional advice if needed to make informed investment decisions.
- _____
  ____ (Specific action to take)
- _____

RETIREMENT ACTION PLAN WORKSHEET

____ (Specific action to take)

1. Lifestyle Design:

- Envision and design the retirement lifestyle that aligns with your goals and aspirations.
- Identify specific activities, hobbies, or experiences you want to pursue.
- _____
  ____ (Specific action to take)
- _____
  ____ (Specific action to take)

1. Health and Wellness in Retirement:

- Recognize the importance of maintaining a healthy lifestyle in retirement.
- Develop a plan for regular exercise, healthy eating, and self-care practices.
- _____
  ____ (Specific action to take)
- _____
  ____ (Specific action to take)

1. Navigating Social Security and Medicare:

- Research and understand the rules and benefits of Social Security and Medicare.
- Evaluate strategies to maximize your benefits.
- _____
  ____ (Specific action to take)

- _____
  ____ (Specific action to take)

1. Legacy Planning:

- Consult with an estate planning professional to create an effective estate plan.
- Consider your wishes for distributing assets and leaving a lasting legacy.
- _____
  ___ (Specific action to take)
- _____
  ____ (Specific action to take)

1. Overcoming Retirement Challenges:

- Anticipate potential challenges in retirement and develop strategies to overcome them.
- Seek support from friends, family, or professionals when needed.
- _____
  ____ (Specific action to take)
- _____
  ____ (Specific action to take)

1. The Power of Networking:

- Identify individuals or groups that can support and provide guidance throughout your retirement journey.
- Attend networking events or join relevant communities to expand your network.

RETIREMENT ACTION PLAN WORKSHEET

- _____
  ____ (Specific action to take)
- _____
  ____ (Specific action to take)

1. Embracing Technology:

- Familiarize yourself with technology tools and resources that can enhance your retirement experience.
- Explore online platforms for financial management, social connections, and learning opportunities.
- _____
  ____ (Specific action to take)
- _____
  ____ (Specific action to take)

1. Travel and Exploration:

- Identify your travel goals and create a budget for travel expenses.
- Research affordable travel options, discounts, and destinations that align with your interests.
- _____
  ____ (Specific action to take)
- _____
  ____ (Specific action to take)

1. Finding Purpose and Meaning:

- Reflect on what gives your life purpose and meaning.
- Explore activities, volunteer opportunities, or projects that fulfill those aspects in retirement.
- _____
  ____ (Specific action to take)
- _____
  ___ (Specific action to take)

1. Retirement and Relationships:

- Evaluate and communicate your expectations with family, friends, and significant others regarding retirement.
- Foster open and supportive communication to maintain healthy relationships during this transition.
- _____
  ____ (Specific action to take)
- _____
  ____ (Specific action to take)

1. Embracing Change and Adaptability:

- Embrace the idea of change and be open to adapting your retirement plan as circumstances evolve.
- Develop strategies to navigate unexpected situations and remain flexible.
- _____
  ____ (Specific action to take)
- _____
  ___ (Specific action to take)

RETIREMENT ACTION PLAN WORKSHEET

Remember, this is a template for you to fill in with specific actions that resonate with your goals and circumstances.

www.ingramcontent.com/pod-product-compliance
Lightning Source LLC
Chambersburg PA
CBHW052313220526
45472CB00001B/94